LEVEL A

MATH
FOR
PROFICIENCY

A Test Preparation Program

GLOBE FEARON
EDUCATIONAL PUBLISHER
A Division of Simon & Schuster
UPPER SADDLE RIVER, NEW JERSEY

Executive Editor: Barbara Levadi
Production Director: Penny Gibson
Project Editors: Bernice Golden, Lynn Kloss, Robert McIlwaine
Production Editor: Nicole Cypher
Marketing Manager: Nancy Surridge
Editorial Developer: Curriculum Concepts, Inc.
Electronic Interior Design: Curriculum Concepts, Inc.
Electronic Page Production: Curriculum Concepts, Inc.
Cover Design: Armando Baéz

Copyright © 1996 by Globe Fearon Educational Publisher, a Division of Simon & Schuster, 1 Lake Street, Upper Saddle River, New Jersey 07458. All rights reserved. No part of this book may be reproduced or transmitted in any form or by any means, electrical or mechanical, including photocopying, recording, or by any information storage and retrieval system without permission from the publisher.

Printed in the United States of America
4 5 6 7 8 9 10   99

ISBN: 0-8359-1840-8

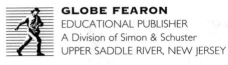

GLOBE FEARON
EDUCATIONAL PUBLISHER
A Division of Simon & Schuster
UPPER SADDLE RIVER, NEW JERSEY

CONTENTS

INTRODUCTION
Succeeding on the Mathematics Test...... 4

CHAPTER 1
NUMBER CONCEPTS AND OPERATIONS

LESSON 1 Using Number Lines to Compare Numbers 6

LESSON 2 Using Equivalent Numbers to Make Comparisons 8

LESSON 3 Using Estimation to Compute 10

LESSON 4 Evaluating Whether an Answer Is Reasonable 12

LESSON 5 Describing the Steps to an Answer 14

LESSON 6 Taking a First Step to Solve a Problem........... 16

LESSON 7 Solving an Easier Problem ... 18

LESSON 8 Making a Model to Picture Relationships 20

Number Concepts and Operations Test.................... 22

CHAPTER 2
MEASUREMENT AND GEOMETRY

LESSON 1 Drawing a Picture 26

LESSON 2 Using Visualization 28

LESSON 3 Using the Process of Elimination 30

LESSON 4 Breaking Down a Problem... 32

LESSON 5 Taking a First Step to Solve a Problem........... 34

LESSON 6 Making a Model 36

LESSON 7	Setting Up a Proportion 38

Measurement and Geometry Test 40

CHAPTER 3
DATA AND STATISTICS

LESSON 1	Isolating Necessary Information 44
LESSON 2	Using the Process of Elimination 46
LESSON 3	Creating a Simpler Problem or Example 48
LESSON 4	Using Visual Estimation 50
LESSON 5	Using Guess and Test 52

Data and Statistics Test............. 55

CHAPTER 4
PATTERNS AND FUNCTIONS

LESSON 1	Making a Table............ 60
LESSON 2	Making a Generalization..... 62
LESSON 3	Using Equivalent Numbers to Find Patterns.......... 64
LESSON 4	Using Ratios and Proportions 66
LESSON 5	Making an Organized List ... 68

Patterns and Functions Test........... 70

CHAPTER 5
ALGEBRA

LESSON 1	Writing and Solving Equations.............. 74
LESSON 2	Using Substitution 76
LESSON 3	Using Guess And Test...... 78

LESSON 4	Using Numerical Examples .. 80

Algebra Test................... 82

CHAPTER 6
CHOOSING A STRATEGY

LESSON 1	Solving Problems with Special Relationships 86
LESSON 2	Solving Problems with Complex Measurements 88
LESSON 3	Solving Problems with Constant Rates or Ratios.... 90
LESSON 4	Solving Problems with Variables................ 92
LESSON 5	Solving Problems When You Can't Use a Calculator 94
LESSON 6	Solving Two-Step Problems 96
LESSON 7	Solving Complex Problems 98
LESSON 8	Solving Problems When You Forget the Procedure.. 100

CHAPTER 7
SOLVING OPEN-ENDED PROBLEMS

LESSON 1	Reading and Solving Open-Ended Problems.... 102
LESSON 2	Exploring and Solving Open-Ended Problems 104
LESSON 3	Practice Solving Open-Ended Problems 106

Solving Open-Ended Problems Test.... 108

Glossary 112

INTRODUCTION

Soon you'll be taking your state's mathematics test. There are several big questions that students wonder about as they prepare for the test. This book is going to answer those questions.

THE BIG QUESTIONS

1. How Can This Book Help Me?

The book is organized around certain strategies that are helpful in solving test problems. By practicing these strategies, you'll learn to recognize the ones that work best for you. Knowing the strategies will build your confidence and improve your speed and accuracy on the test. You will also learn to recognize when to use a certain strategy to solve a test problem.

The concepts and skills needed to solve the problems in this book are the same ones you'll need to do well on your state test. Reviewing these concepts and skills will give you a chance to pinpoint and focus on the areas where you need improvement.

This book will give you practice solving all the types of problems that will be on your state test. The various types of problems include multiple-choice problems as well as open-ended problems that ask you to show your work or explain your answer.

Chapters 1–5 in this book will review all the math on the test and will introduce the strategies that will help you. Chapter 6 will show you which strategies work best in certain situations. Chapter 7 will give you a chance to practice solving open-ended problems.

2. What Will Be on the Test?

- There will be many questions that have a choice of answers. This is the **multiple-choice** part of the test. This part of the test will be scored by totaling the number of problems that you answer correctly. Using strategies will increase your chances of answering more problems correctly. Here is a sample multiple-choice problem:

Cherries sell for $2.79 a pound. Jennie has a bag of cherries that weighs $5\frac{1}{2}$ pounds. Which of these amounts is the approximate price of the bag?

    A. $10.26   **B.** $15.35   **c.** $19.46   **D.** $21.86

- The test may also include problems for which you are asked to write and explain your answers. These problems allow you to show how you think about mathematical problems. These problems are often called **open-ended problems**. Here's an example of an open-ended problem:

Find the average of the set of data below.

96.4;   92.3;   89.9;   98.4

Describe a procedure that you could use to find the average without using decimals. Then compute the average using your strategy.

If your test has open-ended problems, it will be scored by readers. The readers are specially trained to evaluate what you have written. Here are some points the readers will look for in your solutions to problems:

- Is the problem solved completely?
- Is the explanation clear and reasonably correct?
- Does the solution use mathematical language and use appropriate symbols?
- Does the solution show understanding of the math in the problem?

3. **What Do I Have to Do to Get a Good Grade?**

BE PREPARED! To prepare for the multiple-choice test:

- Practice solving the multiple-choice problems at the end of each chapter.
- If you can eliminate some of the answer choices for a problem, make an educated guess. Overall, this will probably improve your score.
- If you forget how to solve a problem, try to think of a new way to solve it. Use the strategies in this book when you get stuck.
- Use estimation to check whether an answer is reasonable.
- Learn how to pace yourself so that you have enough time to finish.

To prepare for the open-ended problem test:

- Practice solving open-ended problems. Some will ask you to find a particular answer. Others will ask you to express an opinion and support it mathematically.
- Learn how to explain your reasoning. Don't just state your answer to a problem—tell how you reached your conclusions.
- Practice using mathematical language and symbols when you explain your work.

You will see this clock on the chapter test pages of this book. It is there to remind you that most math tests are timed. The time on the clock will give you an idea of how much time you would have if you were taking the test.

Now it's time for you to begin preparing for your mathematics proficiency test. Remember, you can do it!

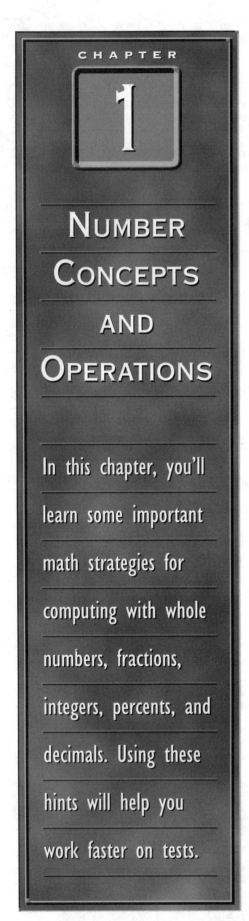

CHAPTER 1

NUMBER CONCEPTS AND OPERATIONS

In this chapter, you'll learn some important math strategies for computing with whole numbers, fractions, integers, percents, and decimals. Using these hints will help you work faster on tests.

USING NUMBER LINES TO COMPARE NUMBERS

All numbers are related to one another. This means that you can **compare** two or more unlike numbers. A *number line* can help you compare two unlike numbers or put a set of numbers in order.

On a math test, you may be asked to compare 3.1 and $3\frac{3}{4}$.

To make a number line, think of the smallest **interval**, or span of numbers, that will contain both numbers.

1. Ask yourself: Are both numbers between 1 and 10? between 1 and 5? between 3 and 4? _____

In this situation you are comparing a decimal and a fraction. Draw fraction and decimal number lines that show the interval you have chosen.

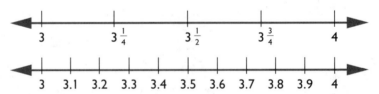

Make a dot at $3\frac{3}{4}$ and at 3.1.

2. Is 3.1 closer to 3 or closer to 4? _____

3. Is $3\frac{3}{4}$ closer to 3 or closer to 4? _____

4. Is $3\frac{3}{4}$ greater or less than $3\frac{1}{2}$? _____

5. What decimal seems equivalent to $3\frac{1}{2}$? Is 3.1 greater or less than that decimal? _____

You can conclude that 3.1 is less and $3\frac{3}{4}$ is greater. You can use the < or > symbol to show this relationship.

$$3.1 < 3\frac{3}{4} \qquad 3\frac{3}{4} > 3.1$$

3.1 is less than $3\frac{3}{4}$ $3\frac{3}{4}$ is greater than 3.1

APPLY

You can also use number lines to help compare **negative numbers**.

Put ⁻5, ⁻8, and ⁻8½ in order from greatest to least.

Complete this number line so that it shows all three numbers.

Think about what the number line shows.

6. Is ⁻8½ to the right of ⁻8 or to the left of ⁻8? Why?
   _____

7. Is ⁻5 to the right of ⁻8 or to the left of ⁻8? Why?
   _____

8. Write the three numbers in order from greatest to least.
   greatest: _____ next greatest: _____ least: _____

PRACTICE

Compare the following groups of numbers. Write each group in order from greatest to least. Make number lines on another paper.

9. $5\frac{1}{4}$ and 5.5 _____

10. ⁻3 and ⁻3.3 _____

11. 7, $7\frac{1}{3}$, and $7\frac{1}{4}$ _____

12. 1, ⁻$1\frac{1}{4}$, and 0.9 _____

13. 20.7, $20\frac{1}{2}$, and 21 _____

THINK ABOUT IT

14. Look back at the group of numbers in Exercise 12 in Practice. Give three numbers that would be between the greatest and the least numbers in that group. One number should be a fraction. One number should be a decimal. One number should be a negative number. List your three numbers in order from greatest to least. _____

15. Tell what you know about the number $\frac{7}{8}$. Which two whole numbers is it between? Which whole number is it closest to? If you made a number line, what are some other numbers that would be close to $\frac{7}{8}$ on the number line?

   _____
   _____

USING NUMBER LINES TO COMPARE NUMBERS

USING EQUIVALENT NUMBERS TO MAKE COMPARISONS

You learned in Lesson 1 that using number lines is a strategy for comparing numbers that are very different, such as 3.1 and $3\frac{3}{4}$. Sometimes, though, you must compare numbers that are close together, such as 2.2 and $2\frac{1}{4}$. In such cases a *better strategy is to rewrite all the numbers as the same kind of number*. For instance, you could rewrite a decimal as an equivalent fraction or a fraction as an equivalent decimal. Then you can easily see which number is greater and which is less.

LEARN

Compare 2.2 and $2\frac{1}{4}$.

You can write both numbers as equivalent fractions.

$$\frac{2}{10} \to \times 2 \to \frac{4}{20}$$

$2.2 \to 2\frac{2}{10} \to 2\frac{4}{20}$ $2\frac{1}{4} \to 2\frac{5}{20}$

$$\frac{1}{4} \to \times 5 \to \frac{5}{20}$$

$2\frac{4}{20}$ is less than $2\frac{5}{20}$

So, $2.2 < 2\frac{1}{4}$

1. Why were both fractions written as twentieths?

_____

Or you can write both numbers as equivalent decimals instead.

$2.2 \to 2.20$ $2\frac{1}{4} \to 2.25$

2.20 is less than 2.25

So, $2.2 < 2\frac{1}{4}$

$$\begin{array}{r} .25 \\ 4\overline{)1.00} \\ \underline{8} \\ 20 \\ \underline{20} \end{array}$$

APPLY

You can also use this strategy in test problems that ask you to compare prices and find the best buy.

Angeline needs to buy buttons for an outfit she is sewing. She sees the following price list for the type of button she wants. Which brand of button is the best buy?

New Look Buttons:	2 dozen for $5.28
Sew-Right Buttons:	1 dozen for $2.88
Fine Look Buttons:	4 for $1.12
Magic-Sew Buttons:	3 for $0.81

OperationsNow.com LEARNING ACTIVITIES

OM EXPLORATION

- Check It Out
- OM in Action
- Online Business Tours
- Letters from the Top
- Putting It All Together: Virtual Case Studies
- Additional Reading

CHAPTER ENHANCEMENT RESOURCES

- Esources
- Reel Operations Video Clips
- Interactive Models
- Excel Tutors
- Supplementary Readings
- Links to Operations On Site Companies

To compare prices, you need to find the cost of the same number of each brand of button. You could find the cost of one button. You could also find the cost of 12 buttons.

2. For which brand do you already know the price of 1 dozen buttons?
_____

3. Find the cost of 1 dozen (12) New Look Buttons. _____

$$\frac{24 \text{ buttons} \rightarrow \div 2 \rightarrow 12 \text{ buttons}}{\$5.28 \rightarrow \div 2 \rightarrow \quad ?}$$

4. Find the cost of 12 Fine Look Buttons. _____

$$\frac{4 \text{ buttons} \rightarrow \times 3 \rightarrow 12 \text{ buttons}}{\$1.12 \rightarrow \times 3 \rightarrow \quad ?}$$

5. Find the cost of 12 Magic-Sew Buttons. _____

$$\frac{3 \text{ buttons} \rightarrow \times 4 \rightarrow 12 \text{ buttons}}{\$0.81 \rightarrow \times 4 \rightarrow \quad ?}$$

6. Which brand has the lowest price for 1 dozen buttons?
_____

PRACTICE

Compare, using the equalizing strategy. Tell which number in each pair is greater.

7. 5.3; $5\frac{1}{3}$ _____ **8.** $2\frac{1}{3}$ dozen; 27 _____

9. .05; $\frac{1}{15}$ _____ **10.** 100 min; $1\frac{3}{4}$ hr _____

11. 6.4; $6\frac{1}{5}$ _____ **12.** 18%; $\frac{1}{8}$ _____

13. Marco wanted to express the decimal 0.721 as a percent. He knew that the correct percent was either 7.21%, 72.1%, or 721%. Which percent should he choose?
_____

THINK ABOUT IT

14. Look back at the problem in Apply. What other number of buttons could you have used to compare prices in the way you did here? Could you have compared 6 buttons? Could you have compared 10 buttons? Could you have compared 36 buttons? Explain.
_____
_____

USING ESTIMATION TO COMPUTE

When you don't need an exact answer, *you can estimate, or make a good guess, to find your answer.* Even when you need to find an exact answer, you can estimate to see whether your answer is reasonable, or makes sense. You can use estimation with any kinds of numbers, including whole numbers, decimals, or fractions. On a multiple-choice test, estimation can also help you eliminate choices that are not reasonable.

Multiply 12.2369 × 3.875. Will your answer be closer to 30, 40, or 50?

To find the exact answer, you have to multiply a 6-digit number by a 4-digit number. These are difficult numbers to work with. So, before you start multiplying, try rounding the numbers to whole numbers.

$$\text{Round } 12.2369 \rightarrow 12 \qquad \text{Round } 3.875 \rightarrow 4$$

$$12 \times 4 = 48$$

1. Based on this result, will your exact answer most likely be closer to 30, 40, or 50? _____

If the whole numbers were still difficult to multiply—for example 42 and 17—you could round to the tens place and multiply 40 × 20. Always round to a place that makes the numbers easy to work with but that still gives the most accurate estimate possible.

An estimate will not always help you decide between two nearly equal answer choices. After an estimate gives you a reasonable answer range, you may still need to find an exact answer.

Divide $166.38 by 3.54.

    A. 32   **B.** 39   **C.** 44   **D.** 47

You can estimate using whole numbers.

$$3.54\overline{)\$166.38} \rightarrow 4\overline{)\$160}\;\;\underset{40}{} \qquad \text{OR} \qquad 3.54\overline{)\$166.38} \rightarrow 3\overline{)\$150}\;\;\underset{50}{}$$

Your estimates tell you that 32 is too small, but in this case, you'll need an exact answer.

$$3.54\overline{)\$166.38}\;\;\underset{47}{}$$

The correct answer is **D**.

APPLY

You can estimate with fractions as well as decimals.

Almonds cost $3.89 a pound. Jonah chooses several bags of almonds and finds that in all, the bags weigh $2\frac{3}{4}$ pounds. He has $10. Can he afford all the almonds, or will he have to put some back?

This problem doesn't ask for an exact answer. You can therefore estimate. Round both the price (a decimal) and the weight (a fraction) to whole numbers.

2. $3.89 → _____

3. $2\frac{3}{4}$ → _____

4. To find the price, will you add, subtract, multiply, or divide? _____

5. Use mental math to solve with your rounded numbers. What is the estimated price of all the almonds? _____

6. Can Jonah afford all the almonds? _____

PRACTICE

Estimate.

7. $36.35 \div 2.7$ _____

8. $4\frac{1}{4} \times \$5.76$ _____

9. $236 - 77$ _____

10. $34\frac{5}{6} + 62.18$ _____

11. $78.578 + 54\frac{1}{3}$ _____

12. 43.6548×29.652 _____

13. Cherries sell for $2.79 a pound. One customer has a bag of cherries that weighs $5\frac{1}{2}$ pounds. Which of these amounts is the approximate price of the bag? _____

    A. $10.26   B. $15.35   C. $19.46   D. $21.86

THINK ABOUT IT

14. Look back at Exercise 13. If you multiply to compute the exact answer, would it make more sense to change $2.79 to a fraction or $5\frac{1}{2}$ to a decimal? Explain your answer.

    _____

    _____

USING ESTIMATION TO COMPUTE

EVALUATING WHETHER AN ANSWER IS REASONABLE

How can you be sure that you have the right answer to a math problem on a test? One way to check an answer is to *see whether it makes sense when you read the problem again*. Here are some other tips for deciding whether an answer is reasonable.

- If you are given several answer choices, look at the greatest and least answers given. You may immediately be able to see that one or both of them are unreasonable.
- After you solve the problem, estimate to see whether your answer is within a sensible range.

LEARN

A package of pens costs $2.39 in one store. People who buy 30 packages get a discount. Carlos thinks that the total price for 30 packages before the discount will be between $55 and $65. Rico thinks that the price will be between $65 and $75. Evan says the price will be between $7 and $7.50.

Whose answer is most reasonable?

If one package costs $2.39, a little more than $2, then 30 packages would cost a little more than 30 × $2, or $60.

1. Based on this information, whose answer can you rule out—Carlos's, Rico's, or Evan's? _____

To decide which of the other answers is correct, you can multiply with the rounded price of $2.40. The number 30 is already a round number. If you have trouble multiplying $2.40 × 30 mentally, break the number up and multiply separately. Then add the products.

$$\$2 \times 30 = \$60$$
$$\$.40 \times 30 = \$12$$
$$\$60 + \$12 = \$72$$

Your estimate, $72, is between $65 and $75.

2. Whose answer is most reasonable? _____

12 • NUMBER CONCEPTS AND OPERATIONS

APPLY

You can also use this strategy when you work with fractions.

Suppose you are asked to find $\frac{5}{8}$ of $124. Will your answer be closer to $140, $100, $70, or $60?

Even before you estimate, you can rule out one answer because it is not reasonable. This answer is $140.

3. Why is this answer not reasonable?

   _____
   _____

4. Is $\frac{5}{8}$ a great deal less than $\frac{1}{2}$, a little less than $\frac{1}{2}$, a little greater than $\frac{1}{2}$, or close to 1? _____

5. Would the most reasonable answer be a number that is less than $\frac{1}{2}$ of $124 or greater than $\frac{1}{2}$ of $124?

   _____

6. Is the total amount closer to $100, $70, or $60? _____

PRACTICE

Put a check mark next to items for which an answer of about 4,300 is reasonable.

7. 110% of 5,000 _____   8. 5% of 4275.99 _____

9. .075 × 4 _____   10. 8,621.37 ÷ 20 _____

11. 71,400 × .06 _____   12. $2\frac{1}{2}$ × 17,000 _____

Circle the letter of the most reasonable answer.

13. 19.75 × 4   A. 90   B. 79   C. 7.9

14. 532 − 367   A. 205   B. 185   C. 165

THINK ABOUT IT

15. Suppose you multiply a 1-digit number (such as 5, 8, or 7) by a 2-digit number (such as 29, 61, or 83). How many digits will the product have? (Hint: What is the smallest product you are likely to get? What is the greatest product you are likely to get?) _____

    A. definitely 2 digits (like 99)   D. either 3 or 4 digits
    B. definitely 3 digits (like 127)   E. either 2, 3, or 4 digits
    C. either 2 or 3 digits

EVALUATING WHETHER AN ANSWER IS REASONABLE • 13

Describing the Steps to an Answer

Sometimes on a math test you are asked to describe the steps needed to solve a problem. You are asked to choose an **expression** that shows all the steps and the order in which to do them. To do this, *break the solution to the problem into steps.* Think about how you would work each step. Then put the steps together.

LEARN

Andy is a photographer. During the past 6 months, he has photographed the state capitol buildings of 21 of our country's 50 states. He wants to find out what percent of the state capitols he has photographed. Which expression could Andy use to find out?

A. $\frac{21}{71} \times 100$ C. $\frac{21}{50} \times 100$ E. $(21 + 50) \times 100$

B. $(\frac{21}{50} + 6) \times 100$ D. $\frac{27}{50} \times 100$ F. not given

A percent is part of a whole. To find a **percent**, you must know the whole and the part.

- 50 represents the total number of states.
- 21 represents part of this total.
- 6 is the number of months Andy has been working on his photos.

> Percent is a part per hundred.

You don't need to know how long Andy has been working on his photos, so you won't use the number 6.

1. What expression can you eliminate as a possible answer? _____

There are three steps to writing the correct expression:

STEP 1 Write an expression to show the fraction of the state capitols Andy has photographed.

STEP 2 Decide how to write a fraction as a percent.

STEP 3 Combine steps 1 and 2 into one expression.

In expression c,

- $\frac{21}{50}$ shows the relationship of the part to the whole.
- To rewrite a fraction or decimal as a percent, you must multiply by 100. The entire expression $\frac{21}{50} \times 100$ shows that process.

Therefore, Andy can use expression c.

APPLY

A jacket that usually costs $119 is on sale at a 20% discount. What expression can you use to find the new reduced price of the jacket?

A. $119 + ($119 × .20)   B. $119 + $\frac{119}{20}$ C. $119 − ($119 × .20)

2. Write 20% as a decimal for computing. _____

3. Write an expression that shows the amount of the discount.

   $119 _____ .20   (+, −, ×, or ÷)

4. Now write an expression for the reduced price with the discount included.

   $119 _____ ($119 _____ .20)

5. What is the letter of the correct expression? _____

PRACTICE

Choose the expression that solves each problem below.

6. A businessman mails out 6 packages that each weigh 14 ounces. He also sends out another package that weighs 9 ounces. What is the total weight of all the packages? _____

   A. (6 × 14) + 9   B. 6 × (14 + 9)   C. $\frac{14}{9}$ + 6

7. Li orders 5 books that each cost $5.40 including tax. The postage charge for the entire order is $2.50. What is the total price? _____

   A. (5.40 + 2.50) × 5   C. (5.40 × 5) + 2.50
   B. (5.40 + 5) × 2.50   D. (5.40 × .05) + 2.50

THINK ABOUT IT

8. Sometimes there is more than one way to solve a problem. Create *two* different expressions for this problem: Find the perimeter of a rectangle that is 8 m long and 5 m wide.

   _____

   _____

Taking a First Step to Solve a Problem

You may read a test problem and find you have trouble figuring out how to begin. Get started by analyzing what the problem tells you. Then *use the numbers or information given in the problem to find any of the numbers or information not given.* Soon you'll have enough information to solve the problem.

This diagram shows a magic square. Adding the numbers in any row, column, or diagonal gives the same sum. All the numbers in this square are positive whole numbers. What is the value of a?

19	a	b
20	18	16
c	d	e

Think about what you know.
- In a magic square, every row, column, or diagonal has the same sum.
- The square shows one complete row.

1. What is the sum of the complete row?   20 + 18 + 16 = _____

Once you have that sum, look for another group of numbers that you can work with. The first column shows two of the three numbers.
   You know that 19 + 20 + c = 54.
   To find c, add 19 + 20 and subtract that number (39) from 54.
$$c = 15$$
Now you can find b by adding the numbers on the diagonal.
   15 + 18 + b = 54
   So, b = 21

> 15 + 18 = 33
> 54 − 33 = 21

2. How will you use b to find a?

_____

   So, a = 14

16 • Number Concepts and Operations

APPLY

Building new information can be a useful approach in many problems that involve money and percents.

Hugh bought a lamp for $30. Including state sales tax, the lamp's total price was $31.50. He wants to buy a rug at the same store for $90. What will the rug's total price be?

Start by thinking about what information is given. Then build on it.

You know that the state sales tax rate is the same for both items.

First find the amount of the sales tax on the lamp. Then find the tax rate.

$31.50 − $30 = $1.50 ⟵ $31.50 is the price including tax. $30 is the price without tax.

To find the tax rate, divide $30)$1.50

3. What percent is the sales tax? _____

Multiply by the tax rate to find the tax on the rug. Then add that amount to the cost of the rug.

$90 $90
× ___   + ___

4. How much will the rug cost in all? _____

PRACTICE

5. Complete the magic square.

160	30	170
	120	

6. Nadine just bought a $20 book. Including tax, she paid $20.80. She has $31 left. Does she have enough money to pay for a $30 textbook that will also have sales tax added? Explain.

_____

THINK ABOUT IT

7. Look back at the problem about the lamp in Apply. What number relationship can you see between the price of the lamp and the price of the rug? How does this relationship help you think of another way to solve the problem?

_____

_____

Solving an Easier Problem

You can sometimes figure out how to solve a test problem by *creating a problem that's similar but easier.* You might even be able to use simpler numbers to figure out the rule that will help you solve a problem.

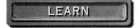

The product of $8^{23} \times 8^{10}$ is either 64^{230}, 64^{33}, 8^{230}, or 8^{33}. Which is the correct product?

Suppose you can't remember the rule for multiplying with **exponents**. You could multiply $8 \times 8 \times 8 \times 8$ and so on to find the value of 8^{23}. Then you could do the same for 8^{10}. This method would take a long time. Instead, try using simpler numbers to see how the problem is worked. Then you can make a rule based on the answer you get.

Try $2^2 \times 2^3$.

First find the values of 2^2 and 2^3.

2^2 is 2×2. 2^3 is $2 \times 2 \times 2$. ⟵ $2 \times 2 = 4$; $2 \times 2 \times 2 = 8$

Then multiply to find the product of $2^2 \times 2^3$.

$4 \times 8 = 32$

Now find the exponent, n, so that $2^n = 32$.

You know that 2^3 is 8. So 2^4 must be 16, and 2^5 must be 32.

So, $2^2 \times 2^3 = 2^5$ ⟵ $2^5 = 2 \times 2 \times 2 \times 2 \times 2 = 32$

> Now you can make a rule:
> **To multiply two numbers with the same base but two different exponents, add the exponents. Do not change the base.**

The correct product of $8^{23} \times 8^{10}$ is 8^{33}.

APPLY

On a test, you may be asked to compare numbers written in different ways. Solving an easier problem can sometimes help you when you need to decide which of these numbers is greater and which is less.

Compare 1.2×10^7 and 100,000.

If you are not sure how to write 1.2×10^7, use a simpler number like 1.2×10^2. You know that $10^2 = 100$.

1. $1.2 \times 100 =$ _____

2. Compare the placement of the decimal in the answer and in 1.2. You moved the decimal point _____ places to the right.

3. Try again with 10^3 to make sure.
   $10^3 = 1000$ $1.2 \times 1000 =$ _____

4. When you multiply 1.2×10^7, how many places to the right will you move the decimal point? _____

5. $1.2 \times 10^7 =$ _____

6. Which is greater, 1.2×10^7 or 100,000? _____

PRACTICE Find the product or the quotient.

7. $52^{33} \times 52^{14} =$ _____   8. $32^{45} \div 32^{44} =$ _____

9. $64^{567} \times 64^{1286} =$ _____   10. $187^{63} \div 187^{61} =$ _____

11. Compare 3.42×10^9 and 342,000. _____

12. In 1992, Taiwan had a population of about 208,000,000. This number was 52 times the population of Luxembourg. What was the 1992 population of Luxembourg?
    A. 40,000,000 people
    B. 4,000,000 people
    C. 400,000 people
    D. 40,000 people

    (Hint: It would be easier to solve this problem by writing the numbers without some of the zeros. Remember to put them back in your answer.) _____

THINK ABOUT IT

13. Suppose you needed to find the **average** of all whole numbers between 1 and 100. What is a simpler problem that would help?

    _____
    _____
    _____

> To find an *average* or *mean* of a group of numbers, add all the numbers. Then divide that sum by the number of numbers in the group.

SOLVING AN EASIER PROBLEM

MAKING A MODEL
TO PICTURE RELATIONSHIPS

If you have trouble figuring out how to solve a test problem, *making a model* can sometimes help. There are many kinds of models. Any model that helps you picture a problem more clearly is a useful tool.

LEARN

Gregorio helped sell raffle tickets. He was given $\frac{1}{5}$ of the total number of tickets to sell. He sold $\frac{7}{8}$ of the tickets he had been given. What fraction of the total number of tickets did he sell?

To solve, you need to multiply $\frac{1}{5} \times \frac{7}{8}$.

If you can't remember how to multiply fractions, you could use a model like this. Divide the entire model into fifths vertically. Also divide the entire model into eighths horizontally.

1. Into how many small sections is the model now divided?

_____

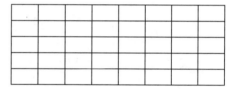

Shade $\frac{1}{5}$ on the model by shading 1 of the 5 rows.

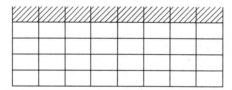

Then, shade $\frac{7}{8}$ on the model by shading 7 of the 8 columns.

Notice the area where the two shaded areas overlap. Count the number of small sections that form that overlapping area.

7 of the 40 sections are in the overlapping area.

So, $\frac{1}{5} \times \frac{7}{8} = \frac{7}{40}$.

Write out your problem: $\frac{1}{5} \times \frac{7}{8} = \frac{7}{40}$

You can see that the answer you got with your model is the same as the product of the two numerators and the product of the two denominators. You can use this rule to multiply other fractions.

APPLY

You can also model the relationship between percents, decimals, and fractions.

Two stores are each having a sale on coats.

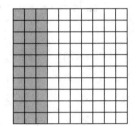

Which discount is greater: 30% or $\frac{1}{4}$?

Use the hundredths model to help you compare the percent and the fraction. Remember that 30% is the same as .30. The model already shows 30% of the squares shaded.

2. How many squares are shaded? _____

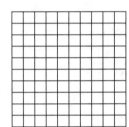

Divide this model into fourths. Shade $\frac{1}{4}$ of the squares.

3. How many squares of the model did you shade? _____

4. Which is a greater discount: 30% or $\frac{1}{4}$? _____

PRACTICE

Use a model to help you solve if you need to.

5. $\frac{5}{6} \times \frac{3}{4} = $ _____

6. $1\frac{1}{2} + \frac{1}{6} = $ _____

7. $4\frac{1}{2} - \frac{2}{3} = $ _____

8. $\frac{7}{8} \times \frac{1}{2} = $ _____

9. Which amount is a greater part of a whole: $\frac{3}{8}$ or 35%? _____

THINK ABOUT IT

10. Look back at Exercise 6 in Practice. What kind of model would be useful for showing addition of fractions? Draw a model here.

CHAPTER 1 TEST

NUMBER CONCEPTS AND OPERATIONS TEST

Use the strategies that you learned in this chapter to help you solve these problems. Use another paper to do calculations or to keep track of your work. Then choose the letter of the correct answer. The clock symbol tells how much time you have to finish the test.

45 MINUTES

1. Which expression is equivalent to $5^3 \cdot 2^4$?
   ⓐ $5 \times 3 \times 2 \times 4$
   ⓑ $5 \times 5 \times 5 \times 2 \times 2 \times 2 \times 2$
   ⓒ $3 \times 3 \times 3 \times 3 \times 3 \times 4 \times 4$
   ⓓ 10×12

2. Which expression is equivalent to $\frac{3^8}{3^4}$?
   ⓐ 3^2
   ⓑ 2
   ⓒ 3^4
   ⓓ 3^{12}

3. The 3-way antenna for Rae's television is broken. Instead of picking up all 9 local stations, Rae picks up only 4. What expression could be used to find the percent of local stations Rae picks up?
   ⓐ $\frac{4}{9} \times 100$
   ⓑ $\frac{(9-3)}{4} \times 100$
   ⓒ $\frac{9}{4} \times 100$
   ⓓ $\frac{7}{9} \times 100$

4. The average distance of Mars from the Sun is 141,600,000 miles. Which of the following represents that figure?
   ⓐ 1.416×10^5
   ⓑ 14.16×10^6
   ⓒ 1.416×10^7
   ⓓ 1.416×10^8

5. Which of the following is equal to 3.562×10^{-5}?
   ⓐ 0.00003562
   ⓑ 0.000003562
   ⓒ $35,630$
   ⓓ $35,620,000$

6. The national debt of the United States in 1970 was 370 billion dollars. Which of the following represents that figure?
   ⓐ $370,000,000
   ⓑ $3,700,000,000
   ⓒ $3,700,000
   ⓓ $370,000,000,000

7. Which of the following fractions is between $\frac{5}{8}$ and $\frac{3}{4}$?
   ⓐ $\frac{5}{9}$
   ⓑ $\frac{11}{16}$
   ⓒ $\frac{1}{2}$
   ⓓ $\frac{4}{5}$

8. Which of the following numbers is between 3.76 and $3\frac{4}{5}$?
   ⓐ $3\frac{3}{4}$
   ⓑ 3.81
   ⓒ 3.79
   ⓓ $3\frac{7}{10}$

22 • NUMBER CONCEPTS AND OPERATIONS TEST

9. What point shown on the number line below could represent the product of $-\frac{1}{4}$ and 6?

   ⓐ point w
   ⓑ point x
   ⓒ point y
   ⓓ point z

10. David claims that the best times to fish for crabs in Texas are during months with the letter r in them. About what percent of the year is this?
   ⓐ 59%
   ⓑ 50%
   ⓒ 75%
   ⓓ 67%

11. Ron recommends that, when erecting a telephone pole, one-fifth of the pole's length should be underground. What part of an 11-meter pole should be underground?
   ⓐ 2 meters
   ⓑ 2.2 meters
   ⓒ 2.4 meters
   ⓓ 5 meters
   ⓔ 6 meters

12. A science exam contains 80 questions. How many questions must be answered correctly to get a score of 65%?
   ⓐ 57   ⓒ 52
   ⓑ 65   ⓓ 61

13. What is 19.38% expressed as a decimal?
   ⓐ 19.38
   ⓑ 0.1938
   ⓒ 0.01938
   ⓓ 1.938

14. Which group of fractions is ordered from greatest to least?
   ⓐ $\frac{3}{5}, \frac{2}{3}, \frac{3}{4}, \frac{1}{2}$
   ⓑ $\frac{2}{3}, \frac{1}{2}, \frac{3}{4}, \frac{3}{5}$
   ⓒ $\frac{1}{2}, \frac{3}{5}, \frac{3}{4}, \frac{2}{3}$
   ⓓ $\frac{3}{4}, \frac{2}{3}, \frac{3}{5}, \frac{1}{2}$

15. The fraction $\frac{1}{16}$ is equal to 0.0625. What is $\frac{7}{16}$ equal to?
   ⓐ 0.7625
   ⓑ 0.4375
   ⓒ 0.3125
   ⓓ 0.5250

16. Federico bought $20\frac{1}{2}$ lb of gravel that costs $.69 a pound and $7\frac{5}{8}$ pounds of gravel that costs $.85 a pound. How many pounds of gravel did Federico buy?
   ⓐ $27\frac{7}{8}$ lb
   ⓑ 28 lb
   ⓒ $28\frac{1}{8}$ lb
   ⓓ $28\frac{1}{2}$ lb
   ⓔ Cannot be determined from information given

17. A recipe for stew calls for $4\frac{7}{8}$ lb of onions. T.J. wants to double this recipe. He has $5\frac{1}{4}$ lb of onions on hand. How many more pounds of onions does he need to buy?
   ⓐ $\frac{3}{8}$ lb
   ⓑ $4\frac{3}{8}$ lb
   ⓒ $4\frac{1}{2}$ lb
   ⓓ $4\frac{5}{8}$ lb
   ⓔ 5 lb

18. If one ostrich egg will serve 24 people for lunch, how many ostrich eggs are needed to serve 408 people?
- ⓐ 14
- ⓑ 15
- ⓒ 16
- ⓓ 17

19. Solve: $25 - 8 + 3 + (^-6) =$
- ⓐ 14
- ⓑ 26
- ⓒ 8
- ⓓ 17

20. Solve: $(^-34) - (^-15) =$
- ⓐ $^-19$
- ⓑ $^-49$
- ⓒ 19
- ⓓ 49

21. Solve: $8 \div (^-2) =$
- ⓐ 4
- ⓑ $^-4$
- ⓒ $-\frac{1}{4}$
- ⓓ $^-16$
- ⓔ $\frac{1}{4}$

22. The following diagram is called a magic square. Adding the numbers in any row or column, or the diagonals will produce the same sum. All of the numbers are positive integers. What is the missing value for e?

d	c	9
e	6	b
3	8	a

- ⓐ 10
- ⓑ 2
- ⓒ 7
- ⓓ 4

23. Which subtraction best shows that 2,876 is a reasonable answer for the difference of 3,592 and 716?
- ⓐ 4,000 minus 1,000
- ⓑ 2,876 minus 716
- ⓒ 3,600 minus 700
- ⓓ 3,592 minus 2,876

24. Robin is buying sour candies that cost $.69 a bag. What is the best way to estimate the cost of 7 bags?
- ⓐ Multiply the cost per bag by the total number of bags
- ⓑ Divide the cost per bag by the total number of bags
- ⓒ Round the cost per bag to the nearest dollar, then multiply by the number of bags
- ⓓ Round the cost per bag to the nearest ten cents, then multiply by the number of bags
- ⓔ Round the number of bags to the nearest ten, then multiply by the cost per bag

25. Clarence is filling a pen with an invisible ink solution. One penful of solution requires $\frac{3}{8}$ oz of lemon juice. How many ounces of lemon juice are needed to fill 13 pens?
- ⓐ $4\frac{1}{2}$ oz
- ⓑ $4\frac{3}{8}$ oz
- ⓒ $4\frac{1}{4}$ oz
- ⓓ $4\frac{7}{8}$ oz

26. The decimal .35 is equal to
- ⓐ $\frac{7}{20}$
- ⓑ $\frac{3}{10}$
- ⓒ $\frac{17}{50}$
- ⓓ $\frac{3}{5}$

27. The decimal .48 is not equal to
    ⓐ $\frac{12}{25}$
    ⓑ $\frac{48}{100}$
    ⓒ $\frac{96}{200}$
    ⓓ $\frac{18}{40}$

28. Matt is planning a 2-day trip for his soccer team. He expects 57 people to eat 3 meals each day. How many servings should Matt plan for?
    ⓐ 114
    ⓑ 171
    ⓒ 285
    ⓓ 342

29. During his trip to Canada, Craig drove 283.5 km the first day, 115 km the second day, 411.3 km the third day, and 87.8 km the fourth day. How many kilometers did Craig drive in all?
    ⓐ 852.6
    ⓑ 842.7
    ⓒ 851.6
    ⓓ 897.6

30. Jupiter, on average, is about 5.203 astronomical units (AU) from the Sun. Mars, on average, is about 1.524 AU from the Sun. On average, how many AU further from the Sun is Jupiter than Mars?
    ⓐ 3.679
    ⓑ 4.321
    ⓒ 5.203
    ⓓ 6.727

31. Which expression could be used to determine the cost of 6 CDs priced at $10.85 each?
    ⓐ $(6 \times 10) + (6 \times 80) + (6 \times 5)$
    ⓑ $(6 \times 10) \times (6 \times .85)$
    ⓒ $(6 + 10) \times (6 + .85)$
    ⓓ $(6 \times 10) + (6 \times .85)$

32. Choose the arithmetic operation that would solve the following problem most easily: If it takes 1 pound of wax to make eight 8-inch candles, how many pounds of wax would it take to make seventy-two 8-inch candles?
    ⓐ multiplication
    ⓑ division
    ⓒ addition
    ⓓ subtraction

33. Ms. Jenkins asked her students to explain why $\frac{7}{8}$ is greater than $\frac{5}{6}$. Which of the following is a correct response?
    ⓐ because the numerator 7 is greater than the numerator 5
    ⓑ because the denominator 8 is greater than the denominator 6
    ⓒ because, on the number line, $\frac{5}{6}$ is further from 0 than $\frac{7}{8}$ is
    ⓓ because, on the number line, $\frac{7}{8}$ is closer to 1 than $\frac{5}{6}$ is

34. Andres wants to know the following: Of the countries that Jessica has visited, what percent are Spanish-speaking? Jessica tells him that she's been to 7 Spanish-speaking countries. What other information does Andres need to answer his question?
    ⓐ The total number of Spanish-speaking countries in the world
    ⓑ The number of Spanish-speaking countries that Jessica has not visited
    ⓒ The total number of countries that Jessica has visited
    ⓓ What percent of Jessica's time was spent visiting Spanish-speaking countries

35. Which of the following statements is true?
    ⓐ $5^2 < \sqrt{25}$
    ⓑ $6 \times \sqrt{16} = \sqrt{4} \times 12$
    ⓒ $3^5 = 5^3$
    ⓓ $4 \times \sqrt{4} = 16 \times \sqrt{16}$

CHAPTER

2

MEASUREMENT AND GEOMETRY

Knowing math strategies can help you think for yourself when you take a math test. The strategies in this chapter will help you make decisions as you solve test problems involving measurement and geometry.

DRAWING A PICTURE

Sometimes a test problem asks for a solution that you have trouble picturing in your mind. *Making a drawing using details from the problem will help you to "see" a problem on paper.* Using a picture to model possible answers or figure out a correct solution is a strategy used by many successful math students.

Point A is located at ($^-$4, 2) on a coordinate plane. If you move point A by 5 units to the right and 3 units down, where will it be located?

You could solve this problem mentally, but a drawing can be very helpful. Create a coordinate grid with an x axis and a y axis. You can draw this grid freehand or with a ruler.

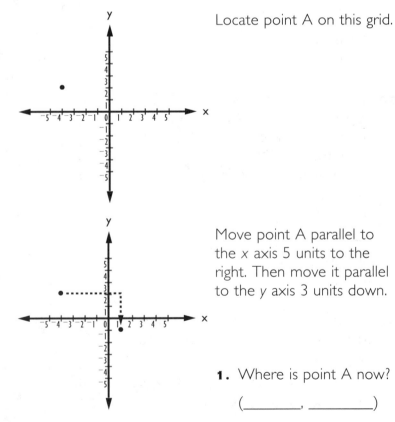

Locate point A on this grid.

Move point A parallel to the x axis 5 units to the right. Then move it parallel to the y axis 3 units down.

1. Where is point A now?

(_____, _____)

26 • MEASUREMENT AND GEOMETRY

APPLY

A water fountain is at the exact center of a rectangle-shaped lawn. The fountain is 15 feet from the north and south edges of the lawn. It is 25 feet from the east and west edges of the lawn. Use the strategy to find the *perimeter* of the lawn.

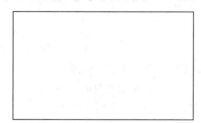

Locate the fountain in the rectangle. Write in the measurements you know from the problem.

2. What is the length of the rectangle? •————— Use the formula $P = 2l + 2w$.
_____

3. What is the width of the rectangle? _____

4. What is the perimeter? _____

PRACTICE

Solve. Make a drawing on another paper if you need to.

5. Jamal draws a circular spinner with 8 equal sections. What size, in degrees, will each section be—
45°, 60°, 90°, or 120°? _____

6. A tool part is made from a flat sheet of metal with a square hole cut in it. The sheet is 16 inches long and 12 inches wide. The hole is 3 inches long and 3 inches wide. How many square inches of metal are used in the tool part? _____

THINK ABOUT IT

7. Look back at Exercise 5 in Practice. What other method besides drawing a picture could you use to solve the problem? (Hint: What do you know about degrees in a circle that could help you?)

_____
_____

DRAWING A PICTURE • **27**

USING VISUALIZATION

Seeing with your mind's eye can help you solve a test problem. For example, you can visually compare the size of two figures or line segments. *Making visual comparisons can help you eliminate answer choices that don't make sense.*

A truck drove 8 miles on a road going east. Then it went 6 miles on a road going south. The truck then drove along side road A back to its starting point. The diagram shows the truck's route. How long is side road A?

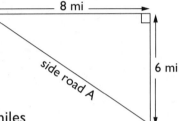

A. 4 miles   **B.** 5 miles   **C.** 10 miles   **D.** 12 miles

Notice in the diagram that the truck's route is a **right triangle**. The corner where two of the roads meet is marked as a right angle.

1. Is side road A a leg or the **hypotenuse**, the longest side, of the right triangle? _____

You can compare the length of side road A to the other roads to estimate its length. You can see that it is longer than each of the other two roads.

2. Based on your visual estimate, which answer or answers do not make sense? _____

3. What is your best estimate of the length of side road A? _____

The **Pythagorean theorem** is the best way to verify your estimate. The **equation** that shows this theorem is $a^2 + b^2 = c^2$. So:

$$6^2 + 8^2 = c^2$$
$$36 + 64 = c^2$$
$$100 = c^2$$
$$\sqrt{100} = c$$
$$10 = c$$

APPLY

The solid shown below has no missing cubes in back. How many cubes are in the solid in all? Using visualization will help you.

A. 7 cubes
B. 11 cubes
C. 9 cubes
D. 13 cubes

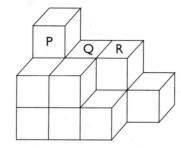

4. First count the cubes you see. Which answer or answers can you eliminate? Why?
   _____

5. Examine cube P. How many cubes are below it in the back row?
   _____

6. How many cubes are below cube Q? _____

7. How many cubes are below cube R? _____

8. Use what you visualized and what you have figured out to arrive at a total number of cubes. _____

PRACTICE

9. These triangles are similar right triangles. What is the length of the shorter leg of the smaller triangle? _____
   A. 14
   B. 16
   C. 20
   D. 24

    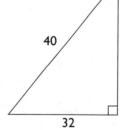

10. Does this solid contain 8 cubes, 9 cubes, 10 cubes, or 11 cubes?

    _____ cubes

    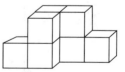

THINK ABOUT IT

11. Look back at the problem in Learn. Carefully examine the numbers that are given. What do you know about a right triangle whose shorter legs measure 3 units and 4 units that could help you solve that problem?
    _____
    _____

USING VISUALIZATION • **29**

Using the Process of Elimination

Often on a test you are asked to choose the correct answer from among several choices. Sometimes you can *begin by eliminating answers that don't make sense based on what you know.* You can often make drawings or use visual clues to help you with this strategy.

Which figure could contain exactly two right angles?

A. a triangle   B. a square   C. a trapezoid   D. a regular pentagon

Use what you know about each figure to eliminate answers.

- A triangle's three angles add up to 180°.
  The sum of *two* right angles is 180°.
  A triangle can't have more than one right angle.

- A square's angles add up to 360°.
  This sum gives room for two 90° angles.
  However, a square always has *four* right angles.

- A regular pentagon has five equal angles that add up to 540°.
  So, each angle is 108°.
  This figure is not a possible answer.

So, the correct figure must be the trapezoid.
To verify your answer, try to picture a trapezoid with two right angles.
One of the other angles would be an acute angle.
The fourth angle would be obtuse.

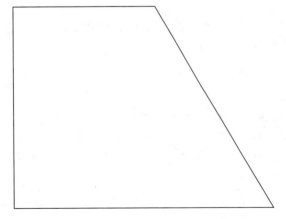

APPLY

The radius of this circle is 21 inches. What is the approximate circumference?

Use $\pi = \frac{22}{7}$. $\frac{22}{7} = 3\frac{1}{7}$

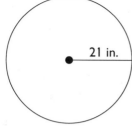

A. 1386 in.   B. 45 in.   C. 66 in.   D. 132 in.

You know that the **circumference** is the distance around the circle. The circumference is also π times the **diameter**, the distance across the circle. The value of π is about 3.

1. What is the diameter of this circle? _____

2. Is answer A a sensible answer? Why or why not?
   _____

3. Look at answer B. If the diameter of a circle is 42 inches, can the entire circumference be 45 inches?
   _____

4. Which of the remaining answers seems to be about 3 times the diameter?
   _____

PRACTICE

Solve. As your first step, eliminate at least one answer that is not sensible.

5. The map shows the road between two cities. You can use a ruler. Is the road between the cities most likely 50 miles, 75 miles, or 125 miles?

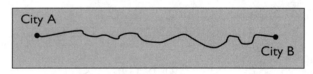

Scale: $\frac{1}{2}$ in. = 25 mi

6. What is the most logical height for a standard office desk: .75 inch, .75 centimeter, .75 meter, or .75 kilometer? _____

THINK ABOUT IT

7. Look back at Exercise 6 in Practice. Which of the possible answers did you eliminate first? Why?
   _____
   _____
   _____

USING THE PROCESS OF ELIMINATION • **31**

BREAKING DOWN A PROBLEM

If a test problem looks too difficult, see whether you can separate it into two or more parts. Solve the parts of the problem separately. Then put the separate elements together. This strategy is especially useful for measuring irregular figures or solids.

The figure shown in the diagram is the same width all along its length. What is its area?

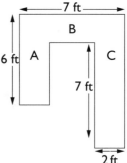

This irregular figure can actually be seen as a group of rectangles. Find the area of each rectangle by using the formula $A = lw$.

You know that Rectangle A is 6 feet long. According to the problem, it's 2 feet wide.

1. The area of Rectangle A is _____ ft².

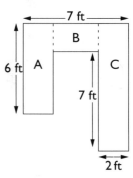

You know that Rectangle C is 2 feet wide. The unknown section of the length of Rectangle C is also the *width* of Rectangle B. So this section must be 2 feet long.

$7 + 2 = 9$ So, Rectangle C is 9 feet long.

2. The area of Rectangle C is _____ ft².

You know that Rectangle B is 2 feet wide. Its length is 7 feet *minus* an unknown length on each side. The missing unknown length is the same as the *width* of Rectangle A and Rectangle C.

$7 - 2 - 2 = 3$ So, Rectangle B is 3 feet long.

3. The area of Rectangle B is _____ ft².

To find the area of the entire figure, add the areas of Rectangles A, B, and C.

4. The area of the entire figure is _____ ft².

32 • MEASUREMENT AND GEOMETRY

APPLY — What is the volume of this solid?

The shaded part of the solid is a cube.

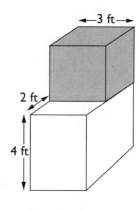

5. What are the length, width, and height of the shaded part?
   _____

$V = s^3$

6. What is the **volume** of the shaded part?
   _____

7. What are the width and height of the unshaded part of the solid?
   _____

8. What numbers will you use to find the length of the unshaded part?
   _____

9. What is the volume of the unshaded part? _____

10. Find the combined volume of the entire solid.

    _____ + _____ = _____

PRACTICE

11. What is the total volume of this solid figure?
    _____

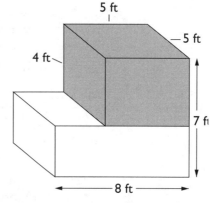

THINK ABOUT IT

12. Look back at the model problem in Learn. Try to divide the figure in a different way. Then draw a diagram to show what you would do. Explain how you would compute the area.

    _____
    _____
    _____
    _____

BREAKING DOWN A PROBLEM • **33**

Taking a First Step to Solve a Problem

Sometimes you come across a test problem that doesn't seem to give enough information. *Look at the details the problem gives you. Use the details to find any new information.* Keep looking for new information until you solve the problem.

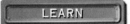

Give the measure of angle F.

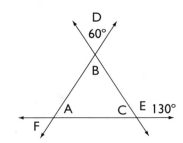

Think about what you already know from the diagram.

- The diagram shows a triangle.
- It gives the measure of two of the triangle's exterior angles.

Here are some facts that will help you find more information.

- The sum of the interior angles of a triangle is always 180°.
- Two angles that share a side and lie along a straight line add up to 180°.
- Vertical angles share a vertex but not a side. They are formed by two intersecting lines. Vertical angles are **congruent**.

Start with the information you have. Try to create new information.

Angle C and angle E share a side and lie along a straight line. Their combined measures add up to 180°.

1. Angle C = _____°

Angle D and angle B are vertical angles. Vertical angles are congruent. So angles B and D have the same measure.

2. Angle B = _____°

A triangle's angles add up to 180°.
angle B + angle C + angle A = 180°

3. Angle A = _____°

> A + B + C = 180
> A = 180 − B − C

Now you have enough information to solve the problem.

Angle A and angle F are vertical angles. Vertical angles are congruent.

4. Since angle A = _____°, angle F = _____° also.

34 • Measurement and Geometry

APPLY

Lines y and z are parallel. What is the measure of angle G?

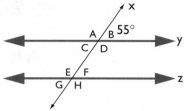

Remember the geometry facts mentioned in this lesson. Here's another fact: If two parallel lines are intersected by a straight line, then the angles in the same position on both lines are congruent.

5. Look at angle B on line y and angle F on line z. How do their positions compare?

   _____

6. What is the measure of angle F? _____ How do you know?

   _____

7. How can you use angle F to help you find the measure of angle G?

   _____

8. What is the measure of angle G? _____

PRACTICE

9. Lines e and f are parallel. Lines g and h are *not* parallel. What is the measure of angle Q?

   _____

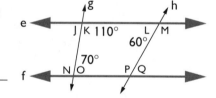

THINK ABOUT IT

10. Suppose you are asked to figure out the measure of angle A in this right triangle. Which detail would be more helpful, the measure of angle D or of angle E? Why?

    _____

    _____

    _____

TAKING A FIRST STEP TO SOLVE A PROBLEM • **35**

MAKING A MODEL

Many test problems ask you to figure out what happens if a figure is moved through space or turned to a different position. It's not always easy to keep track of the movement in your head. Sometimes *making a model* can help you arrive at the correct answer.

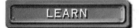

Suppose the figure below is rotated 90° clockwise. Which answer shows the result?

All the answer choices look so similar that it's easy to get confused. Instead of depending on a quick look, act out the problem. Trace the figure on scrap paper. Draw markings on the figure so it looks like the pictured figure.

Then move the figure as the problem directs.

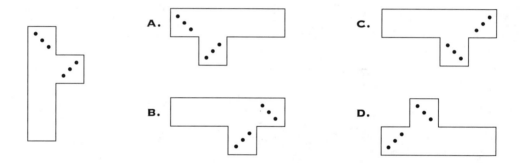

Select the answer that matches your model.

1. Which answer is correct?
   _____

2. If you turn the original figure 90° counterclockwise, which of the answer choices shows the result?
   _____

36 • MEASUREMENT AND GEOMETRY

APPLY

Suppose you rotate this triangle completely around the dotted line. Which figure below shows the correct result?

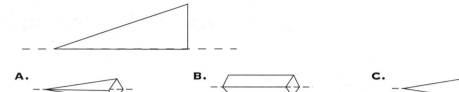

Draw and cut out or tear out a model of the triangle. Stand the triangle up on its base and rotate it. Trace the shape made by the edge of its turn.

3. Is this shape rounded, or does it have angles?

_____

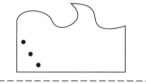

Then stand the triangle on its point and rotate it again.

4. Does the point of the triangle make a shape or remain a point as it rotates?

_____

5. Which answer choice reflects what you have learned from your model?

_____

PRACTICE

6. Flip this figure over the dotted line. Circle the letter of the answer that shows the result.

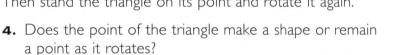

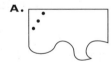 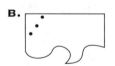 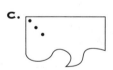

THINK ABOUT IT

7. Look back at the triangle you investigated in Apply. Stand your model up on its base and slide it a short distance along a paper. What solid figure does the slide create?

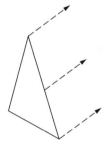

_____

MAKING A MODEL • **37**

Setting Up a Proportion

Often a relationship exists between one set of numbers and another, such as between two units of measurement. When you change units of measure or when you compare similar triangles, *it helps to write a proportion*. A proportion is an expression that shows that two **ratios** are of equal value. An example of a proportion is $\frac{1}{3} = \frac{2}{6}$.

LEARN Triangles ABC and DEF are similar triangles. What is the length of side EF?

Similar triangles, triangles that have the same shape, have sides that are proportional. Use the length of the known sides to create a proportion. In the proportion, compare the long side of one triangle to the long side of the other. Compare the short side of one to the short side of the other. Use a letter to stand for the unknown number.

short side of ABC → $\dfrac{17}{51} = \dfrac{25}{n}$ ← long side of ABC
short side of DEF →   ← long side of DEF

Instead of cross-multiplying with such large numbers as 25 and 51, investigate whether $\frac{17}{51}$ can be reduced to lower terms. Divide 51 ÷ 17.

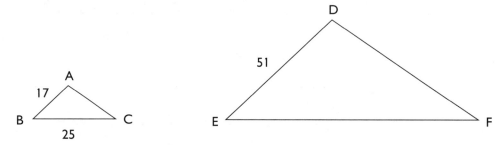

Use your new proportion to solve:

$$\frac{1}{3} = \frac{25}{n}$$

25 × 3 = _____

1. What is the value of *n*? _____

APPLY

Artie's special party punch contains several different kinds of fruit juices. Artie has 16 quart containers of fruit juice. He wants to pour the juice into gallon containers. How many gallons of liquid does he have?

Set up your proportion by deciding what your three known numbers are. Use *n* to stand for the unknown number of gallons of liquid Artie has.

2. How many quarts are in a gallon? _____

   gallons of liquid Artie has → $\dfrac{n}{16} = \dfrac{1}{4}$ ← number of gallons in 1 gallon
   quarts of liquid Artie has →   ← number of quarts in 1 gallon

3. What is the value of *n*? _____

4. How many gallons of liquid does Artie have? _____

PRACTICE

5. Hassan is 6 feet tall and casts an 18-foot shadow. A tree next to Hassan casts an 81-foot shadow. What is the height of the tree? _____

6. Triangles GHI and LMN are similar triangles. What is the length of side MN?

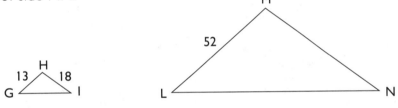

   Length of side MN: _____

THINK ABOUT IT

7. Suppose a diagram shows two triangles. One has a perimeter of 15 in. and a long side that measures 6 in. The other has a perimeter of 30 in. What would you need to know about the triangles before you could use a proportion to find the long side of the larger triangle?

   _____
   _____

8. Suppose a diagram shows two circles. One has a circumference of 44 in. and a radius of 7 in. The other has a circumference of 88 in. Would you need to know any other detail before you could use a proportion to find the radius of the larger circle? Explain.

   _____
   _____

SETTING UP A PROPORTION • **39**

MEASUREMENT AND GEOMETRY TEST

Use the strategies that you learned in this chapter to help you solve these problems. Use another paper to do calculations or to keep track of your work. Then choose the letter of the correct answer. The clock symbol tells how much time you have to finish the test.

45 MINUTES

Use the following figures to answer question 1.

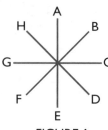

FIGURE 1   FIGURE 2

1. Figure 1 is turned _____ to make Figure 2.
   ⓐ 90° clockwise
   ⓑ 90° counterclockwise
   ⓒ 270° counterclockwise
   ⓓ 45° clockwise

2. There are no missing cubes in the back of this solid. How many cubes make up the figure?

   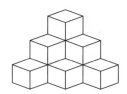

   ⓐ 6
   ⓑ 8
   ⓒ 10
   ⓓ 12

3. The diagram shows part of a circular dartboard that has 20 equal sections. How many degrees of the circle are in each section?

   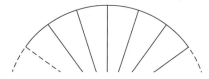

   ⓐ 20°
   ⓑ 16°
   ⓒ 30°
   ⓓ 18°

4. Line k and line l are parallel. What is the measure of angle Y?

   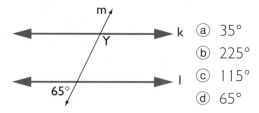

   ⓐ 35°
   ⓑ 225°
   ⓒ 115°
   ⓓ 65°

5. This thermometer's precision allows it to be read to the nearest _____.

   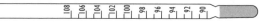

   ⓐ $\frac{1}{2}$ degree
   ⓑ 9 degrees
   ⓒ 2 degrees
   ⓓ 1 degree

6. Which of the following three-dimensional surfaces represents the rotation of rectangle ABCD completely around the dotted line?

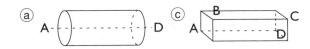

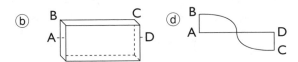

7. The height of an average doorway would be about:
- ⓐ 2.6 centimeters
- ⓑ 2.6 feet
- ⓒ 2.6 yards
- ⓓ 2.6 decimeters

8. The distance from New York City to Buffalo is about 672 kilometers. One mile is about 1.6 kilometers. How could you find the distance, in miles, from New York City to Buffalo?
- ⓐ Divide 672 by 1.4
- ⓑ Multiply 672 by 1.6
- ⓒ Multiply 672 by .6
- ⓓ Divide 672 by 1.6

9. In the circle with center F, what is segment DE called?

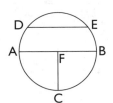

- ⓐ circumference
- ⓑ chord
- ⓒ diameter
- ⓓ radius

10. Shana and Jennie are playing football. Jennie runs straight for 12 yards, turns left, then runs another 5 yards to receive Shana's pass. How far does Shana have to throw the football to reach Jennie?
- ⓐ 10 yards
- ⓑ 12 yards
- ⓒ 13 yards
- ⓓ 15 yards
- ⓔ 17 yards

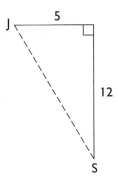

11. Rashid takes the same route to work every day. He works 5 days a week, 49 weeks a year. The distance from Rashid's home to his job is 6 miles one way. Which expression shows the number of miles Rashid commutes to and from work in one year?
- ⓐ (6 × 2) + (5 × 365)
- ⓑ 6 × 5 × 49
- ⓒ 6 × 2 × 49
- ⓓ (6 + 6) × 5 × 49

12. Triangles ABC and RST are similar triangles. How long is side RS?

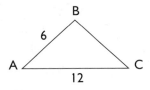 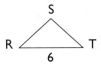

- ⓐ 13
- ⓑ 12
- ⓒ 6
- ⓓ 3

13. Brian's shoulders are 5'7" from the ground. Keisha's shoulders are 4'8" from the ground. Joo is 5'6" tall. How high is the human tower formed by Joo standing on Keisha's shoulders while Keisha is standing on Brian's shoulders?
- ⓐ 16'1"
- ⓑ 15'9"
- ⓒ 14'9"
- ⓓ 13'5"

CONTINUE • 41

14. Mabel won first prize in the dance marathon. She started dancing Wednesday night at 7:30 P.M. and didn't stop until Friday morning at 6:14 A.M. For how long did Mabel dance?

ⓐ 10 hours, 44 minutes
ⓑ 13 hours, 16 minutes
ⓒ 33 hours, 44 minutes
ⓓ 34 hours, 16 minutes
ⓔ 34 hours, 44 minutes

15. Liana bought the safe pictured below. The top, bottom, and sides of the safe are all 1" thick. What is the safe's volume, not counting the walls? (Hint: The inside of the safe is 25" high.)

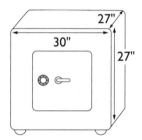

ⓐ 17,500 in.³
ⓑ 18,750 in.³
ⓒ 18,900 in.³
ⓓ 20,412 in.³
ⓔ 21,870 in.³

16. How many centimeters are in 352 meters?

ⓐ 3,250
ⓑ 35,200
ⓒ 3.52
ⓓ 32.2

17. Mustafa drinks 4 pints of water every day. How many cups of water are in 4 pints?

ⓐ 16
ⓑ 4
ⓒ 12
ⓓ 8

18. Triangle XYZ is similar to triangle BCD. What is the length of side YZ?

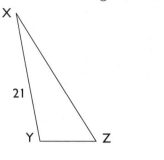
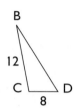

ⓐ 14
ⓑ 7
ⓒ 9
ⓓ 13

19. Mimi is building a rectangular maze for her pet hamster. The outer wall measures 27 inches by 40 inches. What is the perimeter of the outer wall?

ⓐ 67 inches
ⓑ 108 inches
ⓒ 134 inches
ⓓ 160 inches

20. JKL and ABL are similar triangles. What is the measure of angle K?

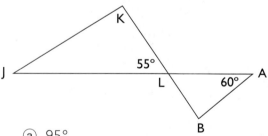

ⓐ 95°
ⓑ 65°
ⓒ 75°
ⓓ 100°

21. In the community park, there is a fountain centered inside a circular path. The distance from the middle of the fountain to the edge of the path is 15 feet. What is the length of the edge of the path?

ⓐ 15π feet
ⓑ 225π feet²
ⓒ 45π feet
ⓓ 15π feet²
ⓔ 30π feet

22. Griselda is $5\frac{1}{2}$ feet tall and casts a 3-foot shadow. A telephone pole next to her casts a 12-foot shadow. What is the height of the telephone pole?

ⓐ $10\frac{1}{2}$ feet
ⓑ $16\frac{1}{2}$ feet
ⓒ 22 feet
ⓓ $23\frac{1}{2}$ feet

23. Which figure contains exactly 2 lines of symmetry?

ⓐ rhombus
ⓑ square
ⓒ trapezoid
ⓓ circle
ⓔ isosceles triangle

24. The instructions for Geeta's aquarium say that the water temperature should fall within a range of 72°–82° Fahrenheit. What is this range in degrees Celsius? (Hint: Use $C = (F - 32) \times \frac{5}{9}$.)

ⓐ 40°–50°C
ⓑ 40°–46°C
ⓒ 32°–42°C
ⓓ 22°–28°C

Use the coordinate plane below to answer question 25.

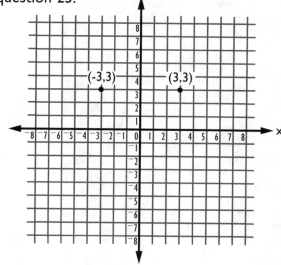

25. Which of the following ordered pairs will form a right triangle when graphed and connected by line segments to the points already on the graph?

ⓐ (0,8)
ⓑ (1,2)
ⓒ (⁻3,⁻1)
ⓓ (4,⁻3)

26. The figure below is 5' wide from one end to the other end. What is the area of the figure?

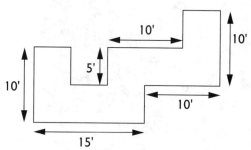

ⓐ 90 ft²
ⓑ 200 ft²
ⓒ 250 ft²
ⓓ 300 ft²
ⓔ 375 ft²

STOP • 43

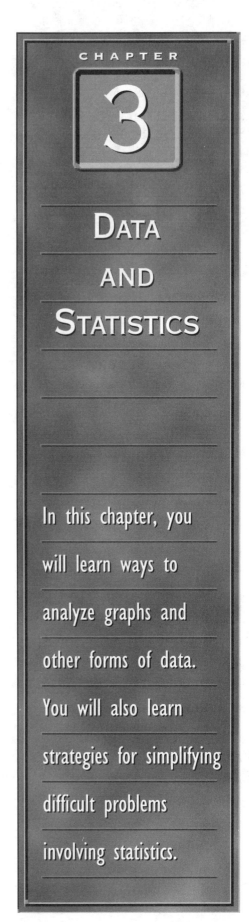

CHAPTER 3

DATA AND STATISTICS

In this chapter, you will learn ways to analyze graphs and other forms of data. You will also learn strategies for simplifying difficult problems involving statistics.

ISOLATING NECESSARY INFORMATION

Graphs and other forms of data often give more information than you need for solving a particular problem. You will need to *isolate the specific information that you need to find the answer*. This strategy is often useful when a problem asks you to compare two pieces of information.

How much would you save if you order a box of 25 thank you cards instead of buying 25 individual cards?

TYPE	INDIVIDUAL	BOX OF 12	BOX OF 25
Holiday Greetings	$1.75	$15.00	$27.00
Children's Birthday	$1.50	$12.50	$21.50
Thank You	$1.25	$10.00	$18.00
Valentine's Day	$1.39	$12.00	$20.00
Special: Box of assorted cards, all types, discontinued designs 50 cards — $15.00			

Read the chart carefully. Locate the information you need.

You know you will need the row that is labeled "Thank You."

1. Which vertical columns contain information you will need?

_____

As you find each detail you need, copy it on a separate part of your paper to keep track of it. If you are working in a test booklet, you can lightly circle or underline the needed details.

Once you have the information you need, you can compute with it.

2. How much would you save by ordering the box of 25 cards instead of 25 individual cards?

_____

```
  $1.25        $31.25
×   25        −$18.00
  625
  250
$31.25
```

44 • DATA AND STATISTICS

APPLY What is the difference between the population of the largest city in Raglan County in 1995 and the largest city in 1955?

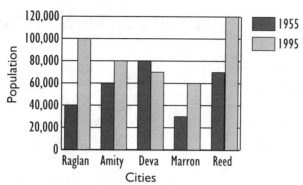

POPULATION OF CITIES IN RAGLAN COUNTY, 1955 AND 1995

3. What was the population of the largest city (the city with the greatest population) in 1995? _____

4. What was the population of the largest city in 1955? _____

5. What will you do to those two numbers to find the answer?
_____

6. What is the difference between the population of the largest city in 1995 and the largest city in 1955? _____ people

PRACTICE

NUMBER OF PAGES ALLOTTED BY SUBJECT					
	Sports	Editorial	Business	Local News	World
The Bailey City News	7.5	2	8.5	15.25	9.5
The Bailey Daily	9	3.25	1.5	20.5	7.25
The Newton Star	6.25	1	2	22	6
The Bailey Times	5	3.5	7.25	18.5	20

7. On average, how much more space do Bailey City's newspapers give to local news than to business news? _____

THINK ABOUT IT

8. Look back at the price list presented in Learn. Write a problem that makes use of the information about how much 50 cards cost.
_____
_____
_____

ISOLATING NECESSARY INFORMATION • **45**

USING THE PROCESS OF ELIMINATION

In some cases, it's easier to tell why a possible answer is wrong than to tell if it's right. *Realizing that one or more answers won't work can help you eliminate unlikely answers.* This will reduce the number of answer choices. Sometimes this strategy will even narrow the possible answers down to just one.

Last month, the Ranchero Hobby Shop sold $2,000 worth of model car kits, $1,500 worth of model airplane kits, and $2,500 worth of action figures. The shop also sells other hobby supplies.

Which graph best represents the data given?

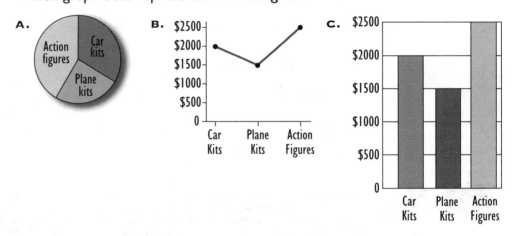

What you know about graphs can help you eliminate answers.

A circle graph such as graph A compares the sizes of parts of a whole. Here the whole is not known. You can eliminate A.

A line graph such as graph B shows trends over a period of time. The data given is not changing over time. You can eliminate B.

This leaves C, the bar graph. Item C is a sensible choice because the purpose of a bar graph is to compare amounts or quantities.

Which statement about the set of numbers below is true?

    68   47   31   32   76   31   29   38   35

A. The *mean* is 80.

B. The *median* is less than the *mode*.

C. The mode and the median are both less than the mean.

46 • DATA AND STATISTICS

1. What answer can you immediately eliminate? Why?
   _____

2. Find the median and the mode. What answer can you eliminate?
   _____

3. Which answer is correct? _____

PRACTICE

4. Based on the chart, which statement is true? _____

SIZES OF PLAYING AREAS IN SOME SPORTS		
Sport	Length	Width
Baseball (infield)	90 ft	90 ft
Bowling	78 ft	41 - 42 in.
Basketball	84 - 94 ft	50 ft
Ice Hockey	200 ft	85 ft
Ultimate Frisbee	360 ft	120 ft

   A. No playing area has a length 3 times its width.
   B. No playing area is larger than 50,000 ft^2.
   C. All playing areas have a length that is different from the width.

5. For a survey, 150 students each named a favorite snack food.

   chocolate — 45
   pretzels — 35
   fresh fruit — 25
   cookies — 15
   chips — 30

   There are 3,000 students in the entire school. Based on the chart figures, what is a good prediction for the number of students out of the entire population whose favorite snack would be pretzels? _____

   A. 3,000   B. 2,000   C. 1,500   D. 700   E. 35

THINK ABOUT IT

6. Look back at Exercise 3 in Apply. What could you do to confirm that your answer is correct?
   _____
   _____

USING THE PROCESS OF ELIMINATION • **47**

CREATING A SIMPLER PROBLEM OR EXAMPLE

Sometimes, the information given in a test problem tells about a whole group of numbers but doesn't tell about each number in the group. This type of information is call **statistics**. You can often make the problem easier to solve by *creating a specific set of numbers to work with*. Other problems are hard because they use numbers that are very complex. In these problems *you can often substitute numbers that are easier to work with*. In both cases, use numbers that accurately fit the information given in the problem.

   Brian's average score on 7 math tests was 78. Then his teacher changed the grade on one of these tests from 83 to 90. What is Brian's average score now?

To find out, you need to create a set of numbers. You know there are 7 tests with an average of 78.

The most obvious set of 7 numbers with an average of 78 is this:

$$78 \quad 78 \quad 78 \quad 78 \quad 78 \quad 78 \quad 78$$

However, you know that one test had a score of 83.
So, *add 5* to one test score to make 83.
Subtract 5 from another test score to keep the average the same.

```
 78    78    78   78   78   78   78
+ 5   − 5
 83    73    78   78   78   78   78
```

1. What is the average of this set of numbers? _____

Now you can change the score of 83 to 90 as the problem directs.

$$90 \quad 73 \quad 78 \quad 78 \quad 78 \quad 78 \quad 78$$

2. What is the total of the 7 scores now? _____

3. What is the new average? _____

APPLY

A set of numbers has a mean of 48, a median of 44, and a range of 51. No two numbers are the same. Suppose you drop the greatest and least number of the set. What statement will be true about the new set of numbers?

    A. The mean will remain the same.

    B. The median will remain the same.

    C. The range will remain the same.

> *Range* is the interval between the greatest number and the smallest number in a set.

Start by finding out how mean, median, and range work in *any* set of numbers. Create two sets of numbers that are easy to work with. (Use two sets to confirm that the process works as a general rule.) As the problem states, no two numbers in a set should be the same. The problem doesn't state how many numbers need to be in the set. Here are some examples:

    SET A: 2   3   5   7   13

    SET B: 10 20 30 40 50

4. What is the mean of each set? Set A: _____ Set B: _____

5. What is the median? Set A: _____ Set B: _____

6. What is the range? Set A: _____ Set B: _____

Remove the greatest and least number from each set.

7. Which remains the same: the mean, the median, or the range?

_____

8. Choose A, B, or C as the answer. _____

PRACTICE

9. Greg has taken 4 history tests so far this term. He knows he will have a 76 average if he gets 83 on the fifth test. Instead, he scores a 93. What is his average score for the 5 tests? _____

THINK ABOUT IT

10. Look back at your answer to Exercise 7. Why do you think this number remained the same while the others changed?

_____

_____

_____

_____

CREATING A SIMPLER PROBLEM OR EXAMPLE

Using Visual Estimation

When you work with graphs, *you can often use what you see to visualize a relationship between pieces of data.* For instance, you can compare sizes of different bars or different circle graph sections. Such comparisons can help you predict or confirm reasonable answers.

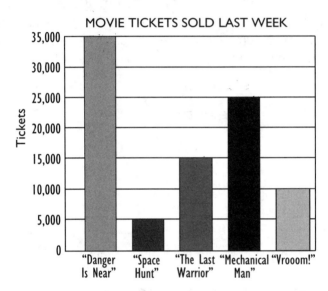

According to the graph, which statement below is true?

   A. *The Last Warrior* was about four times as popular as *Space Hunt*.

   B. *Danger Is Near* was as popular as *Mechanical Man*.

   C. *Mechanical Man* was twice as popular as *The Last Warrior*.

   D. *Space Hunt* was half as popular as *Vrooom!*

Read over the statements as you compare the bars visually.

1. Examine statement **A**. Does the bar for *The Last Warrior* seem four times as long as the bar for *Space Hunt*? _____

2. Look at the bars for the movies mentioned in statements **B**, **C**, and **D**. Which statement or statements can you immediately eliminate? Why?

_____

Statements **C** and **D** remain possible choices. Finding the exact length of each bar will let you make your final choice.

3. Which statement is true? _____

50 • DATA AND STATISTICS

APPLY

Which statement best reflects information from the circle graph?

A. About $\frac{1}{4}$ of the people surveyed prefer running.
B. The number of swimmers is twice the number of runners.
C. The number of people who do aerobics is about the same as the number of people who play team sports.

Favorite Exercise Activity (Survey of 120 people)

4. Does any segment seem to take up $\frac{1}{4}$ of the graph? _____

5. Do any two segments seem to be about equal? _____

6. Does the segment for swimming seem to be about twice the size of the segment for running? _____

7. Which statement is true? _____

PRACTICE

8. Which graph makes all three statements below true?

   • The store's earnings for books are twice as much as its earnings for hobby kits.
   • About $\frac{1}{4}$ of the store's sales in dollars are video games.
   • The store earns an equal amount from its sales of cards and its sales of baby toys.

   _____

A.

B.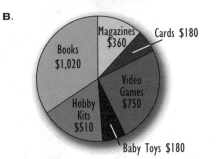

C. Neither graph

THINK ABOUT IT

9. Look back at the circle graphs in Practice. How would you use the numbers given in the graphs to confirm whether your visual estimates led you to the correct answer choice?

_____

USING VISUAL ESTIMATION • **51**

Using Guess and Test

Sometimes the best way to find the correct answer is to choose any one of the possible answers and to test carefully the details that it shows. This *guess and test strategy* is especially useful when the answer to the problem is a table or a graph rather than just a single number.

LEARN

The table shows the cost of parking at the U-Park Lot. Which graph represents the same data?

U-PARK RATES	
up to 1 hour	$2.00
up to 3 hours	$3.00
up to 6 hours	$4.00
over 6 hours	$5.00

A.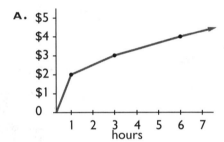

B.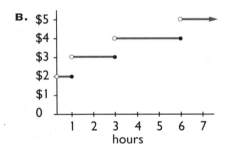

C.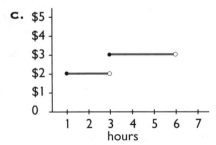

D. None of the graphs

52 • DATA AND STATISTICS

In order to find the right answer, test one amount of time against each graph. For example, the rate for 2 hours is $3.00 (because up to 3 hours costs $3.00).

- On graph A, the rate for 2 hours seems to be about $2.50.
- On graph B, the rate for 2 hours is $3.00.
- On graph C, the rate for 2 hours is $2.00.

Graph B seems like the correct choice. To be sure, try checking other points, such as 5 hours and 7 hours, on the graphs.

APPLY

Geraldo is buying a tape that regularly costs $9.99 and a CD that regularly costs $12.99. The chart shows the discount prices of items in the record store this week. Which advertisement below repeats this discount?

A. 15% off on each item!   C. 10% off today!
B. 25% off!   D. Sale! 20% off!

SALE DAYS!

Regular Price	Discount Price
$13.99	$10.49
$12.99	$9.74
$11.99	$8.99
$10.99	$8.24
$9.99	$7.49

To find the rate of discount, you would have to subtract the discount price from the regular price and then divide the answer by the regular price. This means dividing with three- and four-digit numbers. Since you have four existing answers, it is faster and easier to test each answer. Begin with answer a.

> 15% of $9.99 = *amount of discount*
>
> $9.99 − *amount of discount* = *discount price*

1. What is 15% of $9.99? _____

2. What is 15% of $12.99? _____

3. What do these results tell you about 10% as a possible answer?

_____

4. What will you do next to test possible answers? Why?

_____

_____

5. Which answer choice gives the correct discount prices?

_____

PRACTICE

6. Triangle ABC is a right triangle. The sum of angles B and C is 90°. The chart shows the relationship between Angles B and C in several different specific cases. Which graph represents the same relationship? _____

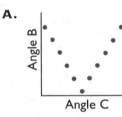

Size of Angles B and C in Right Triangle ABC (A = 90°)	
Angle B	Angle C
80°	10°
70°	20°
60°	30°
50°	40°
40°	50°
30°	60°
20°	70°
10°	80°

7. Which statement best reflects the following spinners? _____

   A. There is a greater probability of spinning 5 on Spinner R and 3 on Spinner S than of spinning 3 on Spinner R and 5 on Spinner S.

   B. There is an equal probability of spinning 5 on either spinner.

   C. There is a $\frac{1}{2}$ probability of spinning an odd number on Spinner R and an even number on Spinner S.

   D. The probability of spinning an even number on Spinner R and an odd number on Spinner S is $\frac{1}{48}$.

SPINNER R

SPINNER S

THINK ABOUT IT

8. Look back at the first problem in Apply, which asks about the tape and CD sale. How could you use what you learn about answer choice C to test answer D? (Hint: Look at the relationship between the two numbers.)

_____

54 • DATA AND STATISTICS

DATA AND STATISTICS TEST

Use the strategies that you learned in this chapter to help you solve these problems. Use another paper to do calculations or to keep track of your work. Then choose the letter of the correct answer. The clock symbol tells how much time you have to finish the test.

45 MINUTES

Use the chart to answer questions 1 and 2.

The Marshall High School planning committee is voting on sites for a school trip. The results of the committee's vote are given below.

Location	Number of votes
Baseball Game	11
Basketball Game	16
Botanical Gardens	8
Beach	12
Amusement Park	13
Total	60

1. The entire school of 1,200 students will vote on the sites next week. Based on the committee's results, what is a good prediction for the number of votes the beach will receive?
   - ⓐ 12
   - ⓑ 100
   - ⓒ 120
   - ⓓ 240
   - ⓔ 500

2. If the basketball game scheduled for the day of the trip was canceled, and the votes divided evenly among the other choices, what percent of the votes would the botanical gardens receive?
   - ⓐ $13\frac{1}{3}\%$
   - ⓑ 20%
   - ⓒ 23%
   - ⓓ $26\frac{2}{3}\%$

3. Sal sold an average of 27 hot dogs per hour over the past 4 hours at his booth at the fair. In the fifth hour, Sal sold 35 hot dogs. Which of the following statements is a reasonable conclusion?
   - ⓐ Every hour Sal sells 8 more hot dogs than he did the previous hour.
   - ⓑ Sal's average is closer to 35 hot dogs per hour than 27 hot dogs per hour.
   - ⓒ Sal's average is closer to 27 hot dogs per hour than 35 hot dogs per hour.
   - ⓓ Sal's new average is 31 hot dogs per hour.

4. Ari has 15 pairs of socks in a laundry bag. Six pairs are gray, 5 pairs are white, 3 pairs are brown, and one pair is red. Ari cannot tell the socks apart by their size or texture. Without looking, he pulls one pair from the bag. What is the probability that the pair of socks chosen is not brown?
   - ⓐ $\frac{1}{5}$
   - ⓑ $\frac{4}{5}$
   - ⓒ $\frac{13}{15}$
   - ⓓ $\frac{4}{15}$

5. Selma and Cyrus are playing a board game that uses the spinner shown. It is Selma's turn to spin. What is the probability that Selma will collect at least $5?
   - ⓐ $\frac{1}{2}$
   - ⓑ $\frac{5}{8}$
   - ⓒ $\frac{3}{4}$
   - ⓓ $\frac{3}{8}$

DATA AND STATISTICS TEST • **55**

6. The graph shows daily attendance figures for 2 baseball teams over a 7-day period. The Flytraps did not play on Wednesday and the Lineshots did not play on Friday.

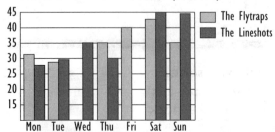

Of the days that both teams played, on which day was the difference in attendance greatest?

ⓐ Sunday   ⓓ Tuesday
ⓑ Thursday   ⓔ Friday
ⓒ Saturday

7. Rolf scored a 62 on his mid-term exam. His score was the lowest in his class. Jaime's score on the same exam was the highest in the class. The median score was 75, the mode was 72, and the range was 23. What was Jaime's score?

ⓐ 78   ⓒ 95
ⓑ 98   ⓓ 85

8. Based on the graph, which conclusion is reasonable?

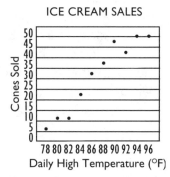

ⓐ Ice cream sales are best when the temperature is 88°.
ⓑ Ice cream sales decrease as the weather gets cooler.
ⓒ Ice cream sales increase as the weather gets cooler.
ⓓ Ice cream sells poorly when the temperature is 92°.

9. A set of data has a mean of 73, a mode of 64, a median of 70, and a range of 22. If the highest and lowest values occur only once, and are deleted from the set, which of the following will definitely change?

ⓐ the mode   ⓓ the mean
ⓑ the median   ⓔ Both B and C
ⓒ the range

Use the circle graph to answer questions 10 and 11.

A soft drink company wants to expand its line of fruit juices. A poll is taken to determine consumer preferences among the proposed new flavors. The graph shows the results of the poll.

Raspberry Mango: 24%
Apple Cherry Lime: 19%
Passionfruit Grape: 38%
Banana Guava: 9%
Kiwi Papaya: 10%

10. One hundred and fifty people were polled. How many voted for Passionfruit Grape?

ⓐ 19   ⓒ 57
ⓑ 39   ⓓ 76

11. How many more people voted for Passionfruit Grape than for Raspberry Mango?

ⓐ 21   ⓒ 28
ⓑ 19   ⓓ 14

Use the graph below to answer questions 12 and 13.

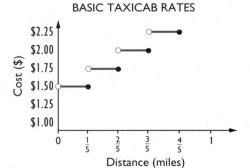

12. Which rate represents the information on the graph?

ⓐ 50¢ for the 1st $\frac{1}{5}$ mile; 25¢ for each additional $\frac{1}{5}$ mile

ⓑ 25¢ for each $\frac{1}{5}$ mile

ⓒ $2.25 for each $\frac{1}{5}$ mile

ⓓ $1.50 for the 1st $\frac{1}{5}$ mile; 25¢ for each additional $\frac{1}{5}$ mile

13. What would be the rate for 2 miles?

ⓐ $2.75   ⓒ $3.75
ⓑ $3.25   ⓓ $5.00

14. For breakfast, Dawn had 2 eggs, 2 slices of bacon, half of a large grapefruit, and 2 cups of black coffee. How many calories were contained in Dawn's breakfast?

FOOD	CALORIES
Orange juice (1 cup)	112
Coffee, black (1 cup)	3
Butter (1 pat)	50
Egg (1)	81
Bacon (2 slices)	97
Grapefruit ($\frac{1}{2}$ large)	104
Cereal (1 cup)	110
Milk, skim ($\frac{1}{2}$ cup)	40
Bread, white (1 slice)	63

ⓐ 282 calories   ⓒ 424 calories
ⓑ 369 calories   ⓓ 476 calories

15. Desiree's scores on her science tests this year were 87, 92, 81, and 93. What must she score on the final test to give her an average of exactly 90?

ⓐ 89
ⓑ 90
ⓒ 93
ⓓ 97
ⓔ She would have to score over 100

Use the tax table to answer question 16.

If your taxable income is-		Single	Married filing jointly	Married filing separately	Head of a household
At least	But less than			Your tax is-	
23,000					
23,000	23,050	3,490	3,454	3,977	3,454
23,050	23,100	3,504	3,461	3,991	3,461
23,100	23,150	3,518	3,469	4,005	3,469
23,150	23,200	3,532	3,476	4,019	3,476
23,200	23,250	3,546	3,484	4,033	3,484
23,250	23,300	3,560	3,491	4,047	3,491
23,300	23,350	3,574	3,499	4,061	3,499
23,350	23,400	3,588	3,506	4,075	3,506
23,400	23,450	3,602	3,514	4,089	3,514
23,450	23,500	3,616	3,521	4,103	3,521
23,500	23,550	3,630	3,529	4,117	3,529
23,550	23,600	3,644	3,536	4,131	3,536

16. Keith is calculating his income tax. He is single and his taxable income is $23,517. Keith has already sent in a tax payment of $1,500. How much tax does Keith still owe?

ⓐ $2,029   ⓒ $2,116
ⓑ $2,017   ⓓ $2,130

Use the table to answer question 17.

LIFETIME STATISTICS				
Baseball Player	Games Played	Home Runs	Batting Average	Hall of Fame
Henry Aaron	3,298	755	.305	1982
Hank Greenberg	1,394	331	.313	1956
Heinie Manush	2,009	110	.330	1964
Zack Wheat	2,410	132	.317	1959
Sam Crawford	2,517	97	.309	1957

17. Which of these players has all of the following characteristics?

—Elected to the Hall of Fame before 1970

—Lifetime batting average over .310

—Hit over 200 home runs

ⓐ Henry Aaron
ⓑ Hank Greenberg
ⓒ Heinie Manush
ⓓ Zack Wheat
ⓔ Sam Crawford

18. The heart rate of an average human at rest is about 72 beats per minute. The graph shows Isamu's heart rate over the course of an hour.

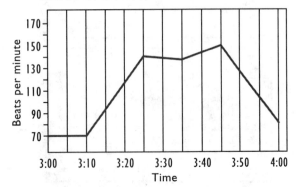

Which of the following statements can be supported by the information on the graph?

ⓐ Isamu was doing light exercise at 3:00, took a nap between 3:10 and 3:40, then went running until 4:00.

ⓑ Isamu was resting at 3:00, went running between 3:10 and 3:40, then settled down to read a book until 4:00.

ⓒ Isamu was resting at 3:00, took a brisk walk at 3:10, took a nap between 3:25 and 3:45, then went running until 4:00.

ⓓ Isamu was resting between 3:00 and 3:40, then went running from 3:40 to 4:00.

Use the graph to answer questions 19 and 20.

On his way to school, Duncan recorded the different colors of suits he observed people wearing. The graph shows his results.

COLOR	
Orange	
Blue	X X X X X X X X
Black	X X X X
Brown	X X X X X X
White	X X X
Tan	X X X X
Green	X X
Yellow	X
Purple	X

19. Of the suits that Duncan observed, what percent were black?

ⓐ 4%

ⓑ 6%

ⓒ $16\frac{2}{3}\%$

ⓓ 20%

20. Which of the following statements is true?

ⓐ Duncan observed 4 times as many green suits as blue suits.

ⓑ Duncan observed more brown suits than white and tan suits combined.

ⓒ Duncan observed half as many tan suits as black suits.

ⓓ Duncan observed $2\frac{1}{2}$ times as many black suits as green suits.

Use the table to answer questions 21–-23.

MOVIES ATTENDED IN THE LAST MONTH									
Number of movies	0	1	2	3	4	5	6	7	8 or more
Number of students	3	2	7	4	3	6	0	1	2

21. How many students went to the movies more than 5 times?

ⓐ 3

ⓑ 12

ⓒ 15

ⓓ 23

22. What number of movies did the most students attend last month?

ⓐ 8

ⓑ 5

ⓒ 4

ⓓ 2

ⓔ 3.1

23. Which graph correctly represents the information given in the table?

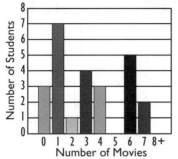

ⓐ MOVIE TICKETS SOLD LAST WEEK

ⓑ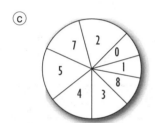

ⓒ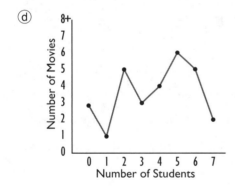

ⓓ

Use the mileage chart to answer question 24.

	Aurora	Meridian	Halfmoon
Aurora	0	4	9
Meridian	4	0	13
Halfmoon	9	13	0

24. Which map gives a possible order for the three towns listed on the mileage chart?

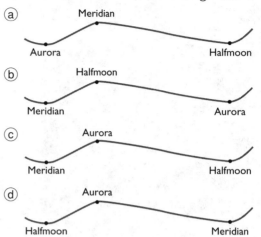

Use the table to answer question 25.

DIMENSIONS OF SQUARES						
Length (in units)	1	2	3	4	5	6
Width (in units)	1	2	3	4	5	6

25. Which graph correctly represents the relationship shown in the table?

ⓐ

ⓑ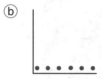

ⓒ

ⓓ

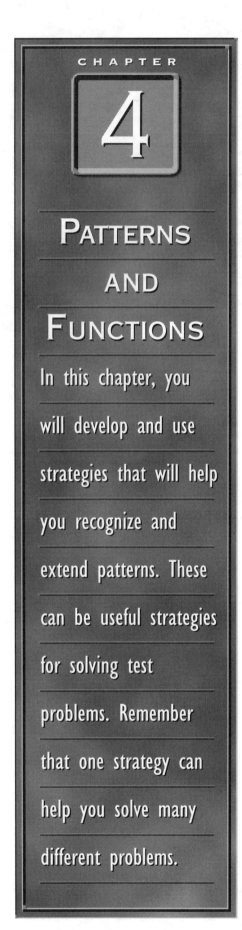

CHAPTER 4

PATTERNS AND FUNCTIONS

In this chapter, you will develop and use strategies that will help you recognize and extend patterns. These can be useful strategies for solving test problems. Remember that one strategy can help you solve many different problems.

MAKING A TABLE

You can often find an unknown number by *making a table*. You can use the table to look for a pattern or a relationship among the given data. Understanding this relationship can help you find the solution.

Ticket prices at the county fair have increased each year in the past four years. Starting at $7.95, prices went to $8.50, then to $9.00, and finally to $9.45. If the price continues to increase in the same manner, what will a ticket cost the sixth year?

You can organize the given prices into a table. Then you'll be able to look for a pattern or number sequence.

YEAR	TICKET PRICE	INCREASE
Year 1	$7.95	
Year 2	$8.50	
Year 3	$9.00	
Year 4	$9.45	
Year 5	?	
Year 6	?	

Use the table to look for a pattern that you can use to solve the problem.

1. How much did the ticket price increase from Year 1 to Year 2? from Year 2 to Year 3? from Year 3 to Year 4?

_____

Think about what the pattern shows:
- The first price increase was $.55.
- Each increase has been $.05 less than the previous year's increase.

60 • PATTERNS AND FUNCTIONS

2. Based on the pattern, how much will the price increase from Year 4 to Year 5? from Year 5 to Year 6?

___

Use the pattern to solve the problem. If the pattern continues, in Year 5 a ticket will cost $9.45 + $.40 = $9.85

3. What will a ticket cost in Year 6? ___

APPLY

Each term in one number sequence is 2.5 more than the term just before it. The first term in the sequence is −11. What is the fourth term?

4. Complete the table to show the sequence.

5. What is the fourth term? ___

TERM	NUMBER
1st term	−11
2nd term	
3rd term	
4th term	

PRACTICE

Make a table to solve the following problems. Use a separate sheet of paper if necessary.

6. Meadowhill High School started with 604 students in 1994. Since then, about 20 fewer students have enrolled each year. About how many students should the principal expect in 1999?

___

7. Mariko rode 12 miles in 15 minutes in the first hour of a bike trip. At this rate, how long will it take her to ride the 36 miles to her destination?

___

8. Zach is training for a bicycle race. Each week for 3 weeks, he doubles the mileage he bikes. If he biked 15 miles the first week, how far did he bike the third week?

___

THINK ABOUT IT

9. Look back at the problem in Apply. How would you find the sixth term in the sequence?

___

10. Look over Exercise 8 in Practice. Write another problem using the same information.

___
___

MAKING A TABLE • 61

MAKING A GENERALIZATION

Finding a pattern—with or without a table—is one way to solve a problem. But sometimes other strategies can be more useful. For example, suppose a test problem asks you to find the 50th term in a sequence. In this case you can find the first few terms in the pattern. Then you can *make a **generalization**, or general statement*, about the pattern. You can use the generalization to solve the problem.

What is the digit in the 30th decimal place of the repeating decimal 0.3589?

You could make a table to find the 30th decimal place. However, this would be time-consuming. It is quicker and easier to look for a pattern in the digits.

.3589 means .35893589...

Dec. Place:	1	2	3	4	5	6	7	8	9
Digit:	3	5	8	9	3	5	8	9	3

Look for a pattern that you can use to make a generalization.

1. How often does the digit 9 occur? _____

From this pattern, you can make the generalization that the digit 9 occurs in every fourth decimal place. For example, it occurs in the fourth decimal place and the eighth decimal place.

2. Think: What decimal place is a multiple of 4 *and* close to the 30th decimal place? _____

Then place the digit 9 in the 28th decimal place and use a small table to solve the problem.

Dec. Place:	28	29	30
Digit:	9	3	5

The solution is that the digit 5 is in the 30th decimal place.

3. What digit would be in the 40th decimal place? _____

62 • PATTERNS AND FUNCTIONS

APPLY

Winona's earnings double each day. The first day she earns 1 penny. How much will she earn the 10th day?

4. Look for a pattern. Her earnings can be written as exponents of 2.

   Day 1 = $.01 or .01 × 2^0 (1)
   Day 2 = $.02 or .01 × 2^1 (2)
   Day 3 = $.04 or .01 × 2^2 (2 × 2)
   Day 4 = $.08 or .01 × 2^3 (2 × 2 × 2)
   Day 5 = $.16 or _____

5. Make a generalization. Each day Winona earns _____ as much as she earned the day before. This exponent is _____ less than the given day.

6. Use the generalization to solve the problem. On the 10th day Winona will earn 2 _____ or $_____.

PRACTICE

Use generalizations to solve the following problems. Use a separate sheet of paper if necessary.

7. Use the following table. What will B equal when A = 100? _____

A	1	2	3	4	5
B	3	6	9	12	15

8. If Shaquille drives 66 miles in 2 hours, how far can he drive in 5 hours? _____

9. Which amount of money would reach $1 million first: a $1,000 deposit that has $1,000 added to it every day, or a $10 deposit that doubles every day? On what day would this amount reach or go over $1 million?

   _____

10. What is the digit in the 50th decimal place of the repeating decimal 0.25341? _____

THINK ABOUT IT

11. Look back at Exercise 8. What was the generalization you made? How did you make it?

   _____

   _____

MAKING A GENERALIZATION

Using Equivalent Numbers to Find Patterns

Sometimes you have to compare numbers of different types to look for a pattern or to place them in numerical order. *It helps to put all the numbers into the same form.* For example, you can write all the numbers either as fractions, as decimals, or as scientific notation.

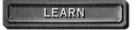

A quiz show lists these numbers in a pattern. To win the grand prize, Dennis has to identify the missing number. This number is given as a percent.

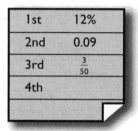

Dennis decides to think of all the numbers as percents since that is the form of the missing number.

He could have chosen to express all the numbers as fractions to hundredths or as decimals if he preferred. After finding the pattern, he would then have converted the missing number to a percent.

$$0.09 = 9\%$$

$$\frac{3}{50} = \frac{6}{100} = 6\%$$

> Think: percent is another way of saying "parts per hundred," so 9% is equivalent to $\frac{9}{100}$.

Dennis's list now looks like this: 12%; 9%; 6%; _____

1. What is the missing percent? Explain how you decided.

_____

2. What if Dennis had chosen to express the numbers in fractional form? What would the pattern have looked like?

_____

64 • PATTERNS AND FUNCTIONS

APPLY

Sometimes when you solve a problem, you must convert your answer to a different unit of measure in order to find the correct answer choice. For example, you may encounter a test problem such as this:

If it takes 25 minutes for Frank to walk 1 mile, how long will it take him to walk 5 miles?

   A. 1 hr 5 min   B. 1 hr 25 min   C. 2 hr 5 min   D. 2 hr 25 min

Find the answer by multiplying 25 × 5 or by making a table.

3. What is the total in minutes? _____

4. Express that total in hours and minutes. •——— 60 min = 1 hr
   _____

5. Which answer choice is correct? _____

PRACTICE

Solve the following problems. Use a separate sheet of paper if necessary.

6. Finish the number pattern, using any form of mathematical notation that you choose:

   $\frac{1}{8}$; 0.25; 0.375; $\frac{1}{2}$; _____ ; _____

7. A recipe for bread uses $1\frac{1}{2}$ cups of milk for every 2 loaves of bread. If Helene plans to bake 10 loaves, how many quarts of milk should she buy? (Hint: 4 cups = 1 quart)
   _____

8. Create a number pattern that begins with 15% and that increases by 0.15 for each item. Show the first six items in the pattern. Express at least two items as fractions reduced to lowest terms and two items as decimals.
   _____

THINK ABOUT IT

9. When you rewrote the numbers in Exercise 6, did you write them as fractions or as decimals? Explain your choice.
   _____
   _____
   _____

USING EQUIVALENT NUMBERS TO FIND PATTERNS • **65**

USING RATIOS AND PROPORTIONS

Some patterns involve numbers that are always in the same ratio or numbers that increase at a constant rate. *You can use proportions to solve problems that involve ratios or rates.* A **proportion** is a sentence stating that two **ratios**, such as $\frac{2}{3}$ and $\frac{4}{6}$, are equal.

LEARN

Mackenzie drove 172 miles in 3 hours. At this rate, how many hours would it take for her to drive 450 miles?

To solve the problem, set up a proportion.

Compare the ratio of miles and hours driven to total miles and total hours.

$$\frac{172 \text{ miles}}{3 \text{ hours}} = \frac{450 \text{ miles total}}{? \text{ hours total}}$$

Write a variable such as T to stand for the total hours.

$$\frac{172 \text{ miles}}{3 \text{ hours}} = \frac{450 \text{ miles}}{T}$$

Solve the proportion.

Cross-multiply
$172 \times T = 3 \times 450$

$$\frac{172 \text{ miles}}{3 \text{ hours}} = \frac{450 \text{ miles}}{T}$$

$172T = 1{,}350$

$T = 7.8488372$ or about 8 hours

APPLY

If Maya earns $25 for 4 hours of work, how much will she earn for a 35-hour work week?

1. Finish the proportion:

   $$\frac{\$25}{4} = \underline{}$$

2. Solve the proportion. How much will she earn for 35 hours of work?

The scale for this drawing of a house is 1 inch:15 ft, meaning that 1 in. in the drawing represents 15 ft in the actual house. What is the length of the house?

3. Finish the proportion to find the length:

   $$\frac{1 \text{ in.}}{15 \text{ ft}} = \underline{}$$

   length of the house = _____ ft

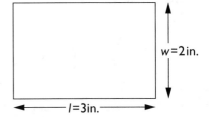

4. Solve the proportion. What is the length of the house?

   _____

5. Write and solve a proportion to find the width of the house.

   _____

PRACTICE

Use ratios and proportions to solve the following problems. Use a separate sheet of paper if necessary.

6. If Luis bikes 18 miles in 3 hours, how many miles will he bike in 7 hours?

   _____

7. The scale for this drawing of a model car is 1 cm: 3.5 cm. What is the length of the actual car?

   _____

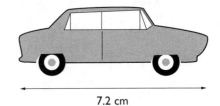

8. Traveling at 25,000 km per hour, a rocket ship travels from Earth to the moon in 16 hours. What is the distance between Earth and the moon? _____

9. If Malik earns $24 for 3 hours' work, how long would he have to work to earn $720? _____

THINK ABOUT IT

10. Use ratios to solve this problem: Which is the better buy, 3 cans for $3.50 or 2 cans for $2.50?

    _____

11. How did you decide?

    _____
    _____

USING RATIOS AND PROPORTIONS • **67**

MAKING AN ORGANIZED LIST

Some problems ask you to find the possible ways that two or more things can be combined. One way to solve these problems is to *make an organized list*.

The following soccer teams are competing in one division. In how many ways can the 4 soccer teams finish in first, second, third, and fourth place? Assume that there are no ties for a place.

Soccer Teams: Arrows   Blazers   Eagles   Mustangs

One way to solve this problem is to make an organized list. Use the first initial to stand for each team. This chart shows the possibilities with the Arrows in first place:

Notice that the list remains orderly to the second and third place.

For example, the two possible arrangements with the Arrows in first place and the Blazers in second place are listed one after the other. This helps you to keep track of which items you have listed.

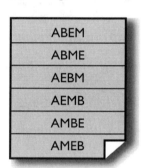

1. List the possible arrangements with the Blazers in first place.

_____

2. List the possible arrangements with the Eagles in first place.

_____

3. List the possible arrangements with the Mustangs in first place.

_____

Then count how many possible arrangements there are in all. You should have 24 possibilities. This is the number of different ways 4 teams can finish in first, second, third, and fourth place.

APPLY   Calla packed 3 pairs of slacks, 2 pairs of shorts, and 4 shirts for a three-day trip. How many different outfits can she wear?

4. Make an organized list. You can assume that Calla wouldn't wear shorts and slacks at the same time, or two shirts at the same time. Let A, B, C, and D stand for the 4 shirts. Let E and F stand for the 2 shorts. Let G, H, and I stand for the 3 slacks.

Outfits with Shirt A: _____

Outfits with Shirt B: _____

Outfits with Shirt C: _____

Outfits with Shirt D: _____

5. Count the possible arrangements. How many different outfits can she put together? _____

PRACTICE

Make an organized list to solve the following problems. Use a separate sheet of paper if necessary.

6. In how many ways can 3 teams finish in a division, assuming that ties for a place are allowed (including a 3-way tie for first place)? _____

7. A chef is planning a banquet menu. Diners may choose soup or salad for the first course; chicken, fish, or pasta for the main course, and strawberries or chocolate cake for dessert. How many possible 3-course dinners are there? _____

8. You are choosing a code to use as a computer password. Here are the rules you must follow:
   - The combination should be made up of two digits.
   - The possible digits are 0, 1, 2, 3, 4, 5, 6, 7, 8, or 9.
   - A digit may *not* be used twice. For example, you cannot use 00, 11, and so on.
   - Digits in a different order become a different possible choice. For example, the combination 12 is one possibility, and the combination 21 is another.

What is the maximum number of combinations from which you can choose? _____

THINK ABOUT IT

9. Look back at the problem in Apply. How would the problem be different if Calla packed 2 hats that could be worn with any outfit instead of 2 pairs of shorts?

_____

_____

PATTERNS AND FUNCTIONS TEST

Use the strategies that you learned in this chapter to help you solve these problems. Use another paper to do calculations or to keep track of your work. Then choose the letter of the correct answer. The clock symbol tells how much time you have to finish the test.

45 MINUTES

1. If the average person burns 1,700 calories resting comfortably for 24 hours, how many calories would an average person burn while resting comfortably for a week?
   - ⓐ 3,400 calories
   - ⓑ 11,900 calories
   - ⓒ 16,800 calories
   - ⓓ 40,800 calories

Use the array to answer questions 2 and 3.

2. What are the missing numbers in the array?

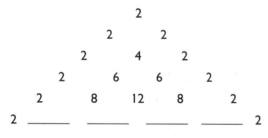

   - ⓐ 8, 12, 12, 8
   - ⓑ 10, 20, 20, 10
   - ⓒ 2, 8, 8, 2
   - ⓓ 10, 12, 12, 10
   - ⓔ 8, 10, 10, 8

3. How many odd numbers will be in the tenth row of the array?
   - ⓐ 10
   - ⓑ 5
   - ⓒ 4
   - ⓓ 0

4. What is the next number in the sequence?
   1, 5, 9, 13, . . .
   - ⓐ 27
   - ⓑ 21
   - ⓒ 19
   - ⓓ 17

5. It takes Theo about 45 minutes to write one page of a term paper. At this pace, how long will it take for him to write a 15-page term paper?
   - ⓐ 6 hours, 45 minutes
   - ⓑ 11 hours, 15 minutes
   - ⓒ 11 hours, 25 minutes
   - ⓓ 15 hours, 45 minutes

6. Each term in a numerical sequence is $1\frac{2}{3}$ times the number before it. The first number in the series is 1. What is the third term?
   - ⓐ 5
   - ⓑ $4\frac{17}{27}$
   - ⓒ $3\frac{1}{3}$
   - ⓓ $2\frac{7}{9}$
   - ⓔ $1\frac{2}{3}$

70 • PATTERNS AND FUNCTIONS TEST

7. Start from the point (⁻4,⁻5) on the coordinate grid. If you plot points by increasing the x coordinate by 1 and the y coordinate by 2, at what point will you cross the y axis?

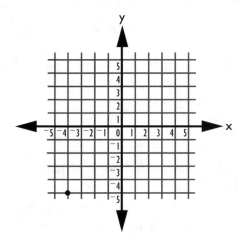

   ⓐ (1,2)
   ⓑ (3,0)
   ⓒ (0,3)
   ⓓ (0,⁻5)
   ⓔ (0,⁻3)

8. Kiri is using a photocopier to reduce a 10" × 16" image. If the length of the image is reduced from 16" to 5", what will be the width of the reduced image?

   ⓐ 8"
   ⓑ 7"
   ⓒ $3\frac{1}{5}$"
   ⓓ $3\frac{1}{8}$"

9. In 1986, Jarvis paid $5.99 for a new cassette. In 1988, he paid $6.99 for a new cassette and in 1990, he paid $7.99. At this rate, what will a new cassette cost Jarvis in 1998?

   ⓐ $9.99
   ⓑ $10.99
   ⓒ $11.99
   ⓓ $13.98

10. Pavel has 23 books in his collection. If he adds 4 books to his collection each month, how many books will he have after 15 months?

    ⓐ 60
    ⓑ 83
    ⓒ 92
    ⓓ 107

11. Olivia works part-time at a pet store. Last month she sold 45 lizards and 25 gerbils. What is the ratio of lizards sold to gerbils sold?

    ⓐ $\frac{5}{14}$
    ⓑ $\frac{9}{5}$
    ⓒ $\frac{5}{9}$
    ⓓ $\frac{14}{5}$

12. What is the next expression in this series?

    $2x, 4x^2, 8x^3, ?$

    ⓐ $10x^4$
    ⓑ $6x^2$
    ⓒ $10x^5$
    ⓓ $16x^4$

13. In the repeating decimal $0.\overline{831549}$, what is the digit in the 40th decimal place?

    ⓐ 8
    ⓑ 3
    ⓒ 1
    ⓓ 5
    ⓔ 4

14. The ratio of catfish to tiger barbs in Ian's aquarium is 3:4. If there are 21 fish in the aquarium, how many are catfish?

    ⓐ 9
    ⓑ 7
    ⓒ 16
    ⓓ 12

15. Jill uses the following guide when buying a refrigerator: Allow 8 cubic feet of space for 2 people. Allow 1 additional cubic foot for each additional person using the refrigerator. Using this method, how much space is appropriate for a refrigerator that will be used by a family of 6?

ⓐ 6 cubic feet
ⓑ 8 cubic feet
ⓒ 10 cubic feet
ⓓ 12 cubic feet
ⓔ 24 cubic feet

16. Students at Stanley High School can take either chemistry or physics for 11th grade science. The ratio of students taking chemistry to students taking physics is 3 to 1. This means:

ⓐ For every student taking chemistry, there are 3 students taking physics.
ⓑ For every student taking physics, there are 3 students taking chemistry.
ⓒ For any 3 students taking 11th grade science, 1 student is taking physics.
ⓓ For any 3 students taking 11th grade science, 1 student is taking chemistry.

Use the table to answer questions 17 and 18.

Radius	A = πr²	Area of circle with radius r
r = 1	π(1)²	π
r = 2	π(2)²	4π
r = 3	π(3)²	9π
r = 4	π(4)²	16π
r = 5	π(5)²	25π
r = 6	π(6)²	36π

17. What happens to the area of a circle when you double the radius?

ⓐ The area becomes 2 times as large.
ⓑ The area becomes 3 times as large.
ⓒ The area becomes 4 times as large.
ⓓ The area becomes 5 times as large.

18. By what factor does the area of a circle increase if you triple the radius?

ⓐ 9   ⓒ 3
ⓑ 6   ⓓ 2

19. Cedric owns 8 T-shirts, 4 pairs of pants, and 3 pairs of sneakers. If he wears one T-shirt, one pair of pants, and one unmixed pair of sneakers, how many different outfits can he make?

ⓐ 15
ⓑ 35
ⓒ 56
ⓓ 96

20. How many 4-digit numbers can be formed with the following characteristics?
—The number must begin with 6 and end with 3
—The number can be formed using the digits 0 through 9
—Each digit can only be used once

ⓐ 100
ⓑ 64
ⓒ 56
ⓓ 63
ⓔ 90

Use the series of figures to answer questions 21 and 22.

21. Which figure comes next in the sequence?

ⓐ   ⓒ

ⓑ   ⓓ

22. What would be the 26th figure in the sequence?

ⓐ   ⓒ

ⓑ   ⓓ

23. Which number is missing from the following series?

$$\frac{1}{2}, \frac{17}{32}, \frac{9}{16}, \underline{}, \frac{5}{8}, \frac{21}{32}, \ldots$$

ⓐ $\frac{20}{32}$
ⓑ $\frac{10}{16}$
ⓒ $\frac{18}{32}$
ⓓ $\frac{19}{32}$
ⓔ $\frac{3}{4}$

24. A certain stock has doubled in value each month over the past 4 months. Four months ago the stock sold for $3.00 a share. How much is one share worth now?

ⓐ $6.00
ⓑ $12.00
ⓒ $24.00
ⓓ $48.00

25. If today is Sunday, what day will it be in 50 days?

ⓐ Sunday
ⓑ Saturday
ⓒ Monday
ⓓ Wednesday
ⓔ Friday

26. The school chess club can send a 4-member team to a state competition. If there are 9 club members, how many different 4-member teams can be formed?

ⓐ 126
ⓑ 36
ⓒ 756
ⓓ 3,024

27. Maryville High School has 2 fencing classes. In one class there are 15 boys and 8 girls. In the other class there are 16 girls and 5 boys. If the classes are rearranged so that the numbers of boys and girls in each class are balanced, what is the ratio of boys to girls in each class?

ⓐ 5:6
ⓑ 6:5
ⓒ 8:5
ⓓ 2:1

28. Boris paid $53.95 for 5 compact discs. The total cost included 8% sales tax. If each disc sells for the same price, what is the total cost of 1 compact disc, including sales tax?

ⓐ $9.99
ⓑ $10.99
ⓒ $11.65
ⓓ $10.79

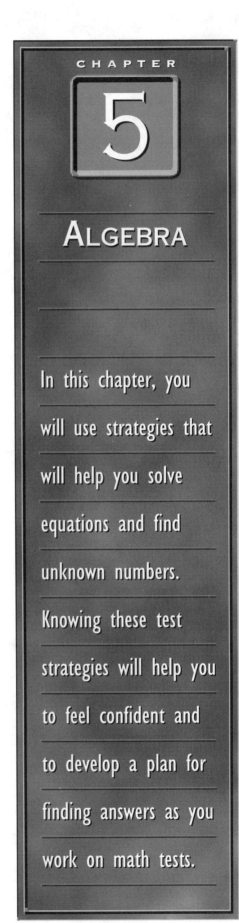

CHAPTER 5

ALGEBRA

In this chapter, you will use strategies that will help you solve equations and find unknown numbers. Knowing these test strategies will help you to feel confident and to develop a plan for finding answers as you work on math tests.

Writing and Solving Equations

Many problems can be solved by *writing and solving an equation* to find an unknown number, or **variable**.

In April, Adventure World hired 128 workers for the summer. This gave the company a total staff of 163 workers. How many people worked for the company before April?

STEP 1 Write an equation. Use variables for the numbers you don't know.

Let p = the workers before April

$p + 128$ = **the total number** of workers

$p + 128 = 163$

STEP 2 Solve the equation by isolating the variable. Subtract 128 from both sides of the equation. This will give you an equivalent equation with the same solution.

$p + 128 = 163$

$p + 128 - 128 = 163 - 128$

$p = 35$

> Always do the *same* thing to *both* sides of an equation.

So, the number of workers before April was 35.

STEP 3 Check your work by substituting 35 in the original equation. To **substitute**, use the number 35 for the variable p.

$p + 128 = 163$

$35 + 128 \stackrel{?}{=} 163$

$163 = 163$ It checks.

APPLY

Last summer Mehmet made three-fifths as much as Sara made. Together, they made $3,250. How much did Sara make?

1. Write an equation:
   $\frac{3}{5}x + x =$ _____, where x = Sara's pay

2. Solve the equation: $\frac{3}{5}x + x = \$3,250$
   $$5(\tfrac{3}{5}x) + 5(x) = 5(\$3,250)$$
   $$3x + 5x = \$16,250$$
   $$8x = \$16,250$$
   $$x = \text{\underline{\hspace{2cm}}}$$

3. Check your work. When you substitute the answer for the variable in the original equation, does the equation remain true? _____

PRACTICE

Solve the following problems. Use a separate sheet of paper.

4. If $^-2n = 34$, what is the value of n? _____

5. Fifty-five less than a number n is equal to the product of 25 and $^-18$. What is the number? _____

6. The Math Club sold raffle tickets for $5 each. After the tickets were sold and $853 was paid for prizes, the club had raised $1,222. How many tickets did the club sell?

   _____

7. During one 92-day period last summer, the City Zoo had 331,734 visitors. The zoo averaged 4,253 visitors for each day it was open. On Mondays the zoo was closed. How many Mondays was it closed? _____

8. What is the value of x in this equation? $\frac{3}{4}x + 7 = 16$ _____

9. Which equation is equivalent to $2x - 150 = 78$? _____
   A. $2x - 150 + 150 = 78 + 150$ C. $\frac{2}{2}x - 150 = \frac{78}{2}$
   B. $2x + 150 = {}^-78$ D. $2x = 78 - 150$

THINK ABOUT IT

10. Write a problem that this equation might be used to solve:
    $^-5 + x = 10$

    _____

    _____

Using Substitution

Sometimes a test will give you a rule of some kind, such as a **function**, a formula, or an inequality. You'll be asked to use the rule to find a missing number. One way to solve these kinds of problems is to *substitute the given number(s) in the rule.*

What number correctly completes the table below?

x	$x^2 + (^-4)$	(x, y)
$^-2$	0	$(^-2, 0)$
0	$^-4$	$(0, ^-4)$
2	0	(2, 0)
8		(8, _____)

The ordered pairs $(^-2,0)$, $(0,4)$, and so on form a *function*.

Use substitution.

In this case, you are being asked to **evaluate**, or find values of, $x^2 + (^-4)$ as part of a function. The quickest way to solve the problem is to substitute 8 for x in the expression: $x^2 + (^-4)$.

1. What is $8^2 + (^-4)$? _____

In another problem, you may be asked to find a missing number in a formula. You can use the substitution strategy here as well.

The formula for simple interest is $I = prt$. *I* means *Interest*, *p* is the *principal*, *r* is the annual *rate* of interest, and *t* stands for the *time* the money is invested.

If you deposit $500 for 6 months at a rate of 7%, how much interest will you earn?

STEP 1 Substitute the given values for the variables in the formula.
  $p = \$500$
  $r = 7\%$ or 0.07
  $t = 6$ months or $\frac{1}{2}$ year or 0.5 years

Since the rate is calculated annually, or yearly, the time must be converted to years.

STEP 2 Evaluate the formula.

2. $I = \$500 \times 0.07 \times 0.5$
  $I = \$$ _____, the interest earned on $500 in 6 months.

76 • ALGEBRA

APPLY

Which of the following ordered pairs is a solution for the inequality $x + 2y \leq 15$?

  A. (0,10)   B. (⁻5,8)   C. (6,5)   D. (⁻1,19)

Substitute the first ordered pair, (0,10), into the inequality:
$$x + 2y \leq 15$$
$$0 + 2(10) \stackrel{?}{\leq} 15$$

$20 \leq 15$ is not true. So, (0,10) is not a solution.

3. Try (⁻5,8). Does the substitution make the inequality true? _____

4. Try (6,5). Does the substitution make the inequality true? _____

5. Try (⁻1,19). Does the substitution make the inequality true? _____

6. Look at your answers. Which ordered pair is a solution for the inequality? _____

PRACTICE

Use substitution to solve the following problems. Use a separate sheet of paper if necessary.

7. What number correctly completes the table at the right?

_____

x	$3x^2$
⁻5	75
0	0
5	75
15	

8. Which of the following ordered pairs is a solution for the inequality: $x + y \leq 7$ _____

  A. (0,6)   B. (3,5)   C. (6,2)   D. (⁻1,9)

9. To convert temperature measurements from Celsius to Fahrenheit, the formula is $F = 1.8C + 32$.

You are in France and the temperature is 15°C. What temperature is that in degrees Fahrenheit?   _____

10. If you deposit $250 for $1\frac{1}{2}$ years at an annual rate of 6.5%, how much interest will you earn?   _____

THINK ABOUT IT

11. Using Exercise 7 as an example, explain how substitution can help you find x if (_____, 48) is part of the table.

_____

_____

USING SUBSTITUTION • **77**

Using Guess and Test

Sometimes you need to solve an equation in a multiple-choice test. It may help to *use one of the answer choices as a guess. Test that guess in the equation.* Even if you choose the wrong number, it will help you decide whether the correct number is less than or greater than the one you chose. This will point you to the most reasonable remaining answer choices.

LEARN

A test might include a problem such as this:
$$40 - 3n = 16$$

What is the value of n?

A. 10   B. 5   C. 12   D. 3   E. 8

Suppose you try 10 as your first guess for *n*.

$$40 - 3(10) \stackrel{?}{=} 16$$
$$40 - 30 \stackrel{?}{=} 16$$
$$10 \neq 16$$

Your first guess shows that *n* is not 10.

Suppose you try $n = 5$.

$$40 - 3(5) \stackrel{?}{=} 16$$
$$40 - 15 \stackrel{?}{=} 16$$
$$25 \neq 16$$

You can now see that *n* is less than 10 but greater than 5. Try a number that is between 5 and 10.

$$40 - 3(\underline{}) \stackrel{?}{=} 16$$
$$40 - \underline{} \stackrel{?}{=} 16$$
$$\underline{} = 16$$

1. What is the correct value of *n*? _____

78 • ALGEBRA

APPLY

You can also use guess and test to solve an equation if you are not given answer choices.

What is the solution for $8x + 12 = 52$?

2. Test a number for x in the equation. What number do you plan to try? _____

   $8 (\underline{\hspace{2cm}}) + 12 \stackrel{?}{=} 52$

   _____

   _____

3. How will you use this first guess to make a second one?

   _____

4. Which value of x is the correct solution? _____

PRACTICE

Use the guess-and-test strategy to solve the following problems. Use a separate sheet of paper if necessary.

5. Find a solution for the following equation: $25 - 3y = 4$ _____

6. Write the value for x that completes the table.

x	1	5	10	
2x − 3	⁻1	7	17	35

7. Which ordered pair on the graph satisfies the equation $y = 2x + 3$?

   _____

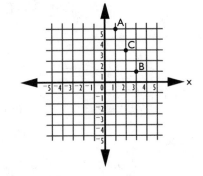

THINK ABOUT IT

8. Use the guess-and-test strategy to find an ordered pair that is a solution of $2x + 3y = 24$. Explain how you found the solution. Can there be another solution?

   _____

   _____

USING GUESS AND TEST • 79

USING NUMERICAL EXAMPLES

Sometimes you will be asked on a test to write an equation that fits a problem with two or more steps. *Substituting specific numbers in the problem can help you determine the relationships in the problem.* You can then write an equation that puts the steps together.

Levar gave $\frac{1}{3}$ of his basketball cards to Marisol. When Marisol added these cards to her 40 cards, she had 72 cards altogether. What equation shows how many basketball cards (c) Levar had at the beginning?

STEP 1 Begin by guessing how many cards Levar had at the beginning: Suppose Levar had 90 cards.

- Find out what $\frac{1}{3}$ of 90 would be:

    $\frac{1}{3}(90) = 30$, the number of cards Levar might have given to Marisol.

- Add this number to the number of cards Marisol already had: $30 + 40 = 70$ cards

- Check this number against the number in the problem:

Since Marisol had 72 cards, this guess for Levar (90 cards) is too low.

STEP 2 Revise your guess, based on the information you discovered from your first guess. Then test it.

1. What if Levar had 96 cards?

    $\frac{1}{3}(96) = 32$ $32 + 40 = $ _____ cards.

STEP 3 Put the two steps together to write the equation.

You know that $\frac{1}{3}(96) + 40 = 72$, the number of cards Marisol has now.

You can then substitute the variable c for the number of cards Levar had (96).

So $\frac{1}{3}c + 40 = 72$ is the equation that can show how to determine the number of cards Levar had at the beginning.

Sometimes using specific numbers can help you write an expression with variables.

What expression represents the total area of the 2 rooms?

80 • ALGEBRA

[Diagram: Bedroom with sides a (left) and b (bottom); Bathroom attached to the right with sides x (bottom) and y (right)]

Choose numerical examples to represent the variables a, b, x, and y. Suppose, for example, that $a = 4$, $b = 5$, $x = 3$, and $y = 2$.

2. Use the numbers to figure out how to find the area (length × width) of the rooms.

Area = (5 × 4) + (_____)

3. Write an expression using the variables a, b, x, and y, rather than the numbers, to represent the total area of the 2 rooms.

Area = _____

PRACTICE

Solve the following problems. Use a separate sheet of paper if necessary.

4. This past summer, Doug made 3 times as much money as he made last summer. This summer he made $1,834. What equation could be used to find how much money Doug made last summer?

_____

5. What expression represents the total area of the 3 rooms? _____

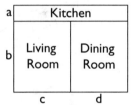

6. A programmer claims her program, SpeedEx, runs $2\frac{1}{2}$ times as fast as her nearest competition. If her competitor's program processes information at a rate of n bytes per second, how many bytes can be processed by the SpeedEx program in 6 seconds? _____

7. Which of the following has the same value as $x(2x + 3)$? _____
   A. $2x^2 + 3$ C. $2x^2 + 3x$
   B. $3x + 3$ D. $6x$

THINK ABOUT IT

8. Look back at Exercise 5. Explain how you used numerical examples to solve the problem.

_____

Algebra Test

Use the strategies that you learned in this chapter to help you solve these problems. Use another paper to do calculations or to keep track of your work. Then choose the letter of the correct answer. The clock symbol tells how much time you have to finish the test.

45 MINUTES

1. A book on aquarium fish suggests that the American Flagfish be kept in water of a temperature within 3 degrees of 71 degrees. Which graph represents this temperature range?

   ⓐ

   ⓑ

   ⓒ

   ⓓ

2. Which of the following has the same value as $2a(a + b)$?
   ⓐ $2a^2 + 2ab$
   ⓑ $2a^2 + 2a + 2b$
   ⓒ $3a + 2ab$
   ⓓ $2a + a^2 + 2ab$

3. Which relationship best describes this table?

x	1	0	⁻1	⁻2	2
y	1	0	1	4	4

   ⓐ $y = x$
   ⓑ $y = {}^-x$
   ⓒ $y = x + 2$
   ⓓ $y = x^2$

4. If $12c - 5 = 31$, what is the value of c?
   ⓐ 3
   ⓑ 2
   ⓒ 14
   ⓓ 24

5. Find the value of m.
   $\frac{m}{2} + 6 = 18$
   ⓐ 9
   ⓑ 6
   ⓒ 12
   ⓓ 24

6. If y is a whole number greater than 6, then $\frac{1}{2}y - 2$ is
   ⓐ greater than 1
   ⓑ less than 0
   ⓒ 1
   ⓓ between 0 and 1

7. Evaluate $(3 - 1)^2 - 5 \times (4 \div 10)$
   ⓐ $\frac{-4}{10}$
   ⓑ 2
   ⓒ 6
   ⓓ $\frac{12}{10}$

82 • Algebra Test

8. If x is the same number in both of the following equations, what is the value of y?

$x - 4 = 3$
$x + y = 4$

ⓐ 3
ⓑ 1
ⓒ 2
ⓓ ⁻3

9. A certain magazine costs $2.50 per issue. If the rising cost of paper drives magazine prices up by 20%, what will the new cost of the magazine be?

ⓐ $2.70
ⓑ $2.75
ⓒ $2.90
ⓓ $3.00

10. Which of the following ordered pairs on the graph does not satisfy the equation $y = 2x - 1$?

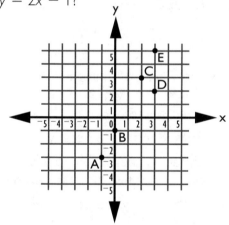

ⓐ A
ⓑ B
ⓒ C
ⓓ D
ⓔ E

11. Which of the following can be described by the equation
$a(b + c) = ab + ac$?

ⓐ $3(4 + 5) = (3)(3) + (4)(5)$
ⓑ $2(8 + 6) = (2)(6) + (2)(8)$
ⓒ $5(2 + 3) = (5)(2) + (5)(3)$
ⓓ $4(9 + 6) = 4 + (9)(6)$

12. Terry suggests that, when planning a chicken coop, you should provide 3 square feet of floor space per chicken. If you had a floor space that measured 6 ft by 9 ft, how many chickens could you accommodate?

ⓐ 54
ⓑ 45
ⓒ 18
ⓓ 5

13. Mr. Powell is an architect. His guide to setting up an office is as follows: Provide 250 sq ft of floor space for each vice-president, 200 sq ft for middle managers, and 175 sq ft for each clerk. Which expression shows the amount of space necessary for c clerks, m middle managers, and v vice presidents?

ⓐ $175v + 250c + 200m$
ⓑ $250v + 175c + 200m$
ⓒ $200c + 175m + 250v$
ⓓ $175c + 250m + 200v$

14. Which equation is equivalent to $5y - 6 = 4$?

ⓐ $5y = {}^-2$
ⓑ $5y - 2 = 3$
ⓒ $5y - 6 + 6 = 4 + 4$
ⓓ $5y - 6 + 6 = 4 + 6$

15. To convert degrees Fahrenheit (°F) to degrees Celsius (°C), the following formula is used:

$°C = (°F - 32) \div 1.8$

What is 104° Fahrenheit in degrees Celsius?

ⓐ 219.2°
ⓑ 129.6°
ⓒ 40°
ⓓ 25.7°

CONTINUE • 83

16. Choose the expression that corresponds with the following statement: Two times a number, n, added to 5.
   ⓐ $2n + 10$
   ⓑ $5 + 2n$
   ⓒ $2(5) + n$
   ⓓ $5n + 2$

17. Choose the expression with the same value.
   $(5 - 2) \times 3$
   ⓐ $15 - 6$
   ⓑ $5 - 6$
   ⓒ $15 - 2$
   ⓓ $5 - 2 \times 3$

18. At the book fair Eng traded away 4 hardcover books for 7 paperback books. He then sold 15 books, bought 8 books, and gave away 2 books. At the end of the day, Eng had 6 books. How many books did Eng start with?
   ⓐ 20
   ⓑ 14
   ⓒ 6
   ⓓ 12

19. Audra makes an average of 148 minutes of business calls every 2 days. At this rate, how much time does she spend making business calls in a five-day work week?
   ⓐ 12 hours 20 minutes
   ⓑ 6 hours 10 minutes
   ⓒ 5 hours 50 minutes
   ⓓ 4 hours 56 minutes

20. Solve for n.
   $\frac{1}{100}n = 3$
   ⓐ 30
   ⓑ $\frac{1}{3}$
   ⓒ $\frac{1}{300}$
   ⓓ 300

21. Val is at the linen store, trying to remember the dimensions of his waterbed. He knows that the bed holds 120 cubic feet of water, is 3 feet high, and is 8 feet long. What is the width of Val's waterbed?
   ⓐ 7 feet
   ⓑ 6 feet
   ⓒ 5 feet
   ⓓ 4 feet

22. Mount Everest is the highest mountain peak in the world, 257 meters higher than the second highest peak, K2. K2 is 8,611 meters high. What equation represents the height, E, of Mount Everest?
   ⓐ $\frac{E}{2} = \frac{8,611}{257}$
   ⓑ $8,611 - 257 = E$
   ⓒ $E - 257 = 8,611$
   ⓓ $E + 257 = 8,611$

23. If x and y are both integers and $x \div y < 0$, then which of the following statements is true?
   ⓐ Both x and y are negative.
   ⓑ Either x is negative and y is positive or x is positive and y is negative.
   ⓒ Both x and y are positive.
   ⓓ More information is necessary to answer the question.

24. It takes Tom 6 hours at an average speed of 60 miles per hour to drive from his home to Tulsa. How far does Tom live from Tulsa?
   ⓐ 100 miles
   ⓑ 600 miles
   ⓒ 360 miles
   ⓓ 60 miles

25. If $2n - p = \dfrac{a}{b}$, what is the value of b?

ⓐ $b = \dfrac{a}{2n - p}$

ⓑ $b = 2\dfrac{n}{a} - p$

ⓒ $b = 2n - \dfrac{p}{a}$

ⓓ $b = a(2n - p)$

26. Jeff estimates that the maximum distance a runner should race is three times the average distance that the runner runs every day. Tomás estimates that a runner shouldn't run a race any longer than one third of his or her weekly training mileage. Which of the following statements is true about Jeff's and Tomás's estimates?

ⓐ Jeff's estimate is greater.

ⓑ The estimates are equal.

ⓒ Tomás's estimate is greater.

ⓓ No comparison can be made from the information given.

27. A parking garage charges $7.25, plus $1.25 for each hour. Which equation could be used to find c, the cost of parking at the garage for t hours?

ⓐ $c = t(7.25 + 1.25)$

ⓑ $c = 7.25 + 1.25t$

ⓒ $c + 1.25 = 7.25t$

ⓓ $1.25c = t + 7.25$

28. Which expression represents the total area of the figure shown?

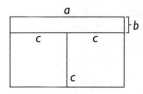

ⓐ $a(b + c)$

ⓑ $c^2 + ab$

ⓒ $ac + bc$

ⓓ $a \times b \times c$

29. Shel works 3 hours a day longer than May. If May works 25 hours in a 5-day work week, how many hours does Shel work each day?

ⓐ 8

ⓑ 7

ⓒ 9

ⓓ 6

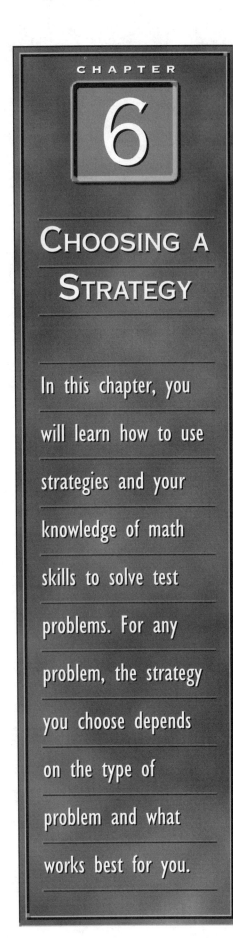

CHAPTER

6

CHOOSING A STRATEGY

In this chapter, you will learn how to use strategies and your knowledge of math skills to solve test problems. For any problem, the strategy you choose depends on the type of problem and what works best for you.

SOLVING PROBLEMS WITH SPECIAL RELATIONSHIPS

Sometimes test problems involve special relationships. A special relationship might be some fact you know such as $\pi = \frac{22}{7}$, or a formula such as $a = \pi r^2$. If you forget the fact or formula, check to see if the test gives you a list of formulas or you can use the information given in the problem to eliminate unreasonable answers. Remember, to solve problems involving special relationships, you can:

- use the special relationships: fact or formula
- *use the process of elimination*

Choose the strategy that you think works better for you.

Here is a problem you might see on a test:

By taxi, the Roxy Theater is 20 blocks east and 15 blocks north of the Museum. Going by subway, what is the distance between the theater and the museum in blocks?

   A. 18   B. 22   C. 25   D. 55

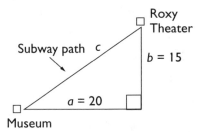

TINA'S STRATEGY: Use special relationships: formula

She knows the formula $a^2 + b^2 = c^2$ where a, b, and c correspond to sides of the triangle. Tina substitutes $a = 20$ and $b = 15$ into the equation and solves for c:

$$20^2 + 15^2 = c^2$$
$$625 = c^2$$

1. The distance c must be _____

86 • CHOOSING A STRATEGY

HORACE'S STRATEGY: Use the process of elimination.

He can't remember the Pythagorean Formula. But he can tell from the diagram that *c* must be larger than *a* or *b*. This rules out choice A, 18 blocks.

From the diagram, Horace can also see that 55 blocks is too long a distance for *c*. This rules out choice D, leaving choices B and C. Horace knows that one of these two choices must be the correct answer. By eliminating choices A and D, he now has a much better chance of choosing the correct answer.

2. Which remaining choice would you rule out? _____

A box is 7 feet long, 4.5 wide, and 5.5 feet high. What is the volume of the box?

　A. 16 cubic ft　　C. 210 cubic ft
　B. 86.6 cubic ft　D. 173.25 cubic ft

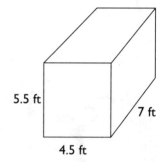

To solve this problem, you need to know the formula for finding volume. If you don't know this formula, you can use the process of elimination.

3. Which strategy will you use? _____

4. What is the volume of the box? _____

5. A sign says the trail to the top of Stratton Mountain measures 8 kilometers. About how far is this in miles?　_____

　A. 20　　B. 5　　C. 62　　D. 14

6. The diameter of a truck tire is 4 feet. What is the distance around the outside of the tire?　_____

　A. 12.56 ft　B. 3.14 ft　C. 50.24 ft　D. 15 ft

7. Jenna has $2\frac{1}{2}$ gallons of sports drink. Into how many individual cup-size servings can she divide the sports drink?　_____

　A. 360　　B. 40　　C. 320　　D. 48

8. The forecast says that today's high temperature will be 15° Celsius. What temperature does this correspond to on the Fahrenheit scale?　_____

　A. 27° C　B. 49° C　C. 99.5° C　D. 59° C

9. How can estimation help you solve a problem when you don't know a formula?

_____

Solving Problems with Complex Measurements

Relationships in test problems can be complicated, especially when measurements are involved. Sometimes you can picture parts of the problem in your mind, but you're not sure how they fit together. Two strategies that can help you are:

- *draw a picture*
- *write an expression that describes the steps to the answer.*

Choose the strategy that you think works best for you.

Below is a problem you might find on a test.

Mark's 30 ft by 20 ft back yard contains a 20 ft by 10 ft inner garden surrounded by a sidewalk. What is the area of the sidewalk?

JOANNA'S STRATEGY: Draw a picture.

She draws this diagram of Mark's yard.

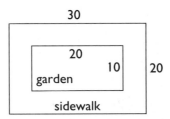

Joanna can see from the picture that the sidewalk must be 5 ft wide all the way around. The area is:

$$(20 \times 5) + (20 \times 5) + (20 \times 5) + (20 \times 5)$$

1. The area of the sidewalk must be _____.

GRAHAM'S STRATEGY: Describe the steps to an answer.

He writes an expression for the area of the back yard and the area of the garden.

$$\text{Area of sidewalk} = \text{Area of yard} - \text{Area of garden}$$
$$= (30 \times 20) - (20 \times 10)$$

2. The area of the sidewalk is _____.

88 • CHOOSING A STRATEGY

APPLY

Freda needs to set up two in-line skating courses. Course 1 is 200 feet long and has one orange cone every 20 feet. Course 2 is 150 feet long and has a cone every 10 feet. How many cones does Freda need in all?

You can draw a picture of how the cones will be set up. Or you can write an expression to represent how many cones Freda will need.

3. Which strategy will you use? _____

4. How many cones does Freda need? _____

PRACTICE

5. Simon shrinks a 12 in by 8 in rectangle in a photocopy machine to a length of 9 inches. What is the width of the shrunken rectangle? _____

   A. 6 inches   C. 14.4 inches
   B. 5 inches   D. 7.5 inches

6. The outside of a safe measures 8 feet by 5 feet by 6 feet. The walls of the safe are 1 foot thick. What is the volume of the inside of the safe? _____

7. A train makes stops in this order: Ashville, Bugtussle, Caraway. The distance from Ashville to Bugtussle is 12 miles. The distance from Ashville to Caraway is 21 miles. What is the distance from Bugtussle to Caraway? _____

8. Jan needs to put tile on a 6 ft by 6 ft square wall. The wall has 4 circular windows that each measure 2 feet in diameter. How much area does Jan need to cover with tile? _____

THINK ABOUT IT

9. Did you use different strategies for problems 5–8? If so, why did you change strategies?

   _____
   _____
   _____

10. Did you use two strategies for the same problem? Explain.

    _____
    _____
    _____

SOLVING PROBLEMS WITH COMPLEX MEASUREMENTS • **89**

SOLVING PROBLEMS WITH CONSTANT RATES OR RATIOS

Problems that involve such topics as travel times or the cost of goods often involve *rates*. When there is a constant rate, you can use several strategies to solve the problem. For example, if you know that the price of each object is the same or that the time needed to travel each mile is the same, your options include:
- *making a table*
- *using multiplication and division*
- *using proportions*

Choose the strategy that you think works best for you.

LEARN

Suppose a test asks: **If lettuce sells at a rate of 2 heads for $3.50, how much will 7 heads of lettuce cost?**

   A. $24.50   B. $16.50   C. $12.25   D. $14.00

GERALD'S STRATEGY: Use a table.

He makes a table to see the pattern. 7 is halfway between 6 and 8 so the cost should be halfway between $10.50 and $14.00.

2	4	6	8
$3.50	$7.00	$10.50	$14.00

1. The cost must be _____.

CARMEN'S STRATEGY: Use multiplication and division.

She starts by finding out how much one head will cost. Then, 7 heads will cost 7 × $1.75

$$\begin{array}{r} \$1.75 \\ \times\ 7 \\ \hline \$12.25 \end{array}$$

$$2\overline{)\$3.50}^{\ \$1.75}$$

WANDA'S STRATEGY: Use a proportion.

She uses proportions because the cost of each head is the same.

$$\frac{2 \text{ heads}}{\$3.50} = \frac{7 \text{ heads}}{n}$$

$$2 \times n = 7 \times \$3.50$$

$$2 \times n = \$24.50$$

$$\frac{2 \times n}{2} = \frac{\$24.50}{2}$$

2. So, $n = $ _____.

APPLY

Rudy, who is 6 ft tall, casts a shadow that is 4 ft long. A nearby tree has a 20 ft shadow. How tall is the tree?

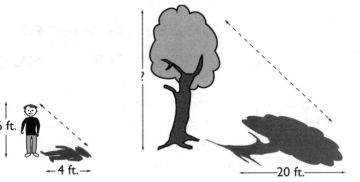

The height of an object and the height of its shadow increase at the same rate. So, you can multiply, use a table, or use a proportion.

3. Which strategy will you use? _____

4. How high is the tree? _____

PRACTICE

5. Louisa is on a bicycling trip. After riding 42 miles in 3 hours, she stops for lunch. If she plans to ride for $4\frac{1}{2}$ hours after lunch, how many additional miles can she expect to ride if she rides at the same rate? _____

   A. 21 miles   C. 105 miles
   B. 63 miles   D. 56 miles

6. Soup is on sale at a rate of 3 cans for $2.00. What is the cost for 11 cans of soup? _____

7. Gear A turns around 6 times when Gear B turns around 8 times. How many times will Gear B turn while Gear A turns 27 times? 1,000 times?

   _____

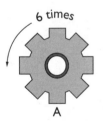 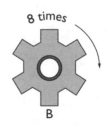

8. The Sharks have won 8 games and lost 4 games so far. They play a total of 30 games. If they continue to win at the same rate, how many games will they win? _____

THINK ABOUT IT

9. Did you use the same strategy for problems 5–8? If so, why?

   _____

10. For which problems does a table work best? Why?

    _____

SOLVING PROBLEMS WITH CONSTANT RATES OR RATIOS • **91**

SOLVING PROBLEMS WITH VARIABLES

Many test problems have equations with variables. To solve the problem, you need to find a number to replace the variable that makes the equation true. To do this, you can:

- *solve the equation*
- *substitute numbers*

Choose the strategy that works better for you.

LEARN

Lauren charges a $200 minimum plus $3.75 per square foot to install a kitchen counter top. She charged $387.50 to do Mr. Green's kitchen. Her price is given by this equation where x stands for square feet of counter top:

$$3.75x + 200 = 387.50$$

Let's say a test question asks: **How many square feet of counter top did Mr. Green have?**

   A. 103.3   **B.** 25   **C.** 50   **D.** 62.5

SPIKE'S STRATEGY: Solve the equation.

He solves for *x*.

$$3.75x + 200 = 387.50$$
$$3.75x + 200 - 200 = 387.50 - 200$$
$$3.75x = 187.50$$
$$\frac{3.75x}{3.75} = \frac{187.50}{3.75}$$
$$x = ?$$

1. In this equation, *x* is equal to _____.

SHAY'S STRATEGY: Use substitution.

She tries different values for *x*, the number of square feet. Each substitution gets her closer to a total of $387.50.

$$3.75(30) + 200 = 312.50$$
$$3.75(60) + 200 = 425$$
$$3.75(45) + 200 = 368.75$$

2. What value for *x* would you choose next? _____

APPLY

Al's Canoe Rentals charges $5 to rent a canoe for the first hour plus $4 for each additional hour. Fernando rented a canoe for several hours and was charged $19. Al used the equation $5 + 4(t - 1) = 19$ to calculate Fernando's bill. If t stands for time, how many hours did Fernando rent a canoe?

You can choose to solve the equation for t. Or you could substitute values into the equation until you come out with a value of 19.

3. Which strategy will you use? _____

4. For how many hours did Fernando rent the canoe? _____

PRACTICE

5. To plan his sailboat cruise, Rex uses the equation $RT = D$, where R is rate, T is time, and D is distance. If Rex sails at an average rate of 15 miles per hour, how long will it take him to travel the 6 miles from Point Baxter to Caper's Cove? _____

   A. 90 minutes   B. $\frac{1}{4}$ hour   C. $\frac{2}{5}$ hour   D. $2\frac{1}{2}$ hours

6. One complete turn of a wheel makes a mark in the sand 15π inches long. Substitute 15π for c into the equation $c = 2\pi r$ to find r, the radius of the wheel. _____

7. A taxi charges $0.75 to enter the cab plus $2.50 for each mile traveled. The cost of a ride is given by the equation: cost $= 0.75 + 2.50m$, where m is the number of miles the cab travels. How far could you ride for $6.75? _____

8. Which solid has the larger volume? _____

$V = (2s)^2 \times h$ $V = \pi(s)^2 \times h$

THINK ABOUT IT

9. Which strategies did you use for problems 5–8? Why did you choose each strategy?

   _____
   _____

10. In Exercise 8, does it matter what values you choose for h and s? Why?

    _____
    _____
    _____

SOLVING PROBLEMS WITH VARIABLES • **93**

SOLVING PROBLEMS WHEN YOU CAN'T USE A CALCULATOR

You may not be allowed to use a calculator on your test. Or you may have forgotten how to complete the calculations needed to find an exact answer. If this happens, you can use estimation. Keep in mind that for almost any test problem, you can:

- calculate exactly
- *use estimation*

Choose the strategy that works better for you.

LEARN

Here is a problem you might see on a test.

Jill got 9.04% simple interest on money she invested last year. The total amount of interest was $27.12. How much money did Jill have invested?

    A. $2.45   B. $275   C. $3,000   D. $300

HANK'S STRATEGY: Calculate exactly

Hank changes 9.04% to a decimal number and then writes an equation:

$$0.0904n = 27.12$$
$$\frac{0.0904n}{0.0904} = \frac{27.12}{0.0904}$$
$$n = ?$$

> 9.04% of what number is $27.12?
> .0904 of n = $27.12

1. The value for *n* is _____.

PIA'S STRATEGY: Use estimation.

Pia forgot how to compute with decimals without using her calculator. So she rounds 9.04% to 10%, then changes 10% to $\frac{1}{10}$. Next, she rounds 27.12 to 30. Then she thinks:

$\frac{1}{10}$ of what number is about 30?

By estimating, Pia can see that choice A above is too small and choice C is too large. This leaves choices B and D. Both are reasonable estimates.

2. Which choice would you make? _____.

APPLY

If $a = 16.2$ and $b = \frac{9}{10}$, what is $\frac{a}{b}$?

   A. 13   B. 20   C. 18   D. 32

If you substitute values for the variables you end up with $16.2 \div \frac{9}{10}$. To simplify this you can divide 16.2 by $\frac{9}{10}$ or simply estimate the answer.

3. Which strategy will you use? _____

4. What solution do you get? _____

PRACTICE

5. What is $3\frac{2}{3}$ % of 700? _____
   A. 25.67   C. 256.7
   B. 28.2   D. 282

6. The list price of a sweater is $62.50. Drake's Department Store sells it for $\frac{7}{12}$ of its list price. How much do they sell it for? _____
   A. $25   C. $40
   B. $26.04   D. $36.46

7. The town of Tyler is 7.5×10^6 cm from the nearest lake. It is 5×10^5 cm from the nearest river. How much closer is the river than the lake? _____
   A. 2.5×10^5 cm   C. 70,000 cm
   B. 7×10^6 cm   D. 7×10^5 cm

8. If $a = ^-4\frac{5}{6}$, what is a^2? _____
   A. 24   C. 23.36
   B. $^-24$ D. $^-23.36$

THINK ABOUT IT

9. Which strategy worked best for problems 5–8? Why did you choose this strategy?
   _____
   _____

10. How can you use estimation to check the exact calculations you made?
    _____
    _____
    _____

SOLVING PROBLEMS WHEN YOU CAN'T USE A CALCULATOR

SOLVING TWO-STEP PROBLEMS

Some test problems have two or more steps. Sometimes you can see how the steps fit together before you start solving the problem. But sometimes you can't. In this case, just try to take a first step. The results of your first step may help you decide what to do next. You can:

- *break down a problem* with a step-by-step plan
- *take a first step* and continue one step at a time

Choose the strategy that works better for you.

LEARN

Bernard walked for 2 hours at 3.5 miles per hour. Then he stopped for 0.5 hours. Then he walked for 0.8 hours at a speed of 4.25 miles per hour. What was Bernard's average speed for the entire trip?

LaShonna's Strategy: Break down the problem.
  Step 1: Find the total distance Bernard walked.
  Step 2: Find the total time that passed.
  Step 3: Divide the total distance by the total time to get the average speed.

Step 1: Total distance: 2 hr × 3.5 mph = 7 miles

0.5 hr × 0 mph = 0 miles

0.8 hr × 4.25 mph = 3.4 miles

Then, 7 + 0 + 3.4 = 10.4 miles

Step 2: Total time: 2 + 0.5 + 0.8 = 3.3 hr

Step 3: Divide total distance by total time.

10.4 miles ÷ 3.3 hr = average speed

1. The average speed is _____.

Jalil's Strategy: Take a first step.

Jalil doesn't have a step-by-step plan. He tries to add the speeds but he realizes that won't work. Then Jalil adds the times together.

2 + 0.5 + 0.8 = 3.3 hr

He uses this to generate new information. He knows that
Rate × Time = Distance so he writes an equation using 3.3 hr for time:

R × (3.3 hr) = D

96 • Choosing a Strategy

Now Jalil can see that in order to solve the equation, he needs to find the total distance traveled. Once he does that he can use the equation he wrote to find R, the average speed.

2. The value of R is _____.

APPLY

Lines m and n are parallel. Find the measure of angle x.

You can develop a step-by-step plan to find the measure of x. Or you can take a first step and fill in the measures of the other angles and see if it leads to a solution.

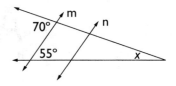

3. Which strategy will you use? _____

4. What is the measure of angle x? _____

PRACTICE

5. Pizza Circus offers a 12 slice pie for $10.00. Jocko's Pizza offers a 9 slice pie for $7.20. Which pizza costs less per slice and how much less does it cost? _____

   A. Circus 9¢   **C.** Jocko's 90¢

   B. Circus 3.33¢   **D.** Jocko's 3.33¢

6. How many ounces are in $4\frac{5}{8}$ gallons of liquid? _____

7. All rows, columns, and diagonals in this magic square add up to 18. Fill in numbers to complete the square.

	8	3
		6

8. One French franc is worth about $0.17. One dollar trades for about 1,200 Italian lire. From this exchange rate, how many lire could you get for 1 franc? _____

THINK ABOUT IT

9. Which of the two strategies did you use more often in problems 5–8? Why did you choose this strategy?

_____

_____

10. Why is it sometimes easier to proceed one step at a time than to make a step-by-step plan?

_____

_____

_____

SOLVING COMPLEX PROBLEMS

At first glance, a problem may seem difficult and complicated. You may need to look at the problem in a new way before you attempt to solve it. Two strategies that help you do this are:
- *write a simpler problem*
- *use guess and test*

Choose the strategy that works better for you.

LEARN

You might see a test problem that looks like this:

A photocopy machine shrinks a picture to 0.833 of its original size. What setting of the machine will bring the picture back to its original size?

    A. .833   **B.** 1.2   **C.** 1.25   **D.** 1.5

HANNA'S STRATEGY: Write a simpler problem.

She makes up a new problem in which the picture shrinks to 0.5, or half of its original size. She then writes an equation:

$$0.5x = 1.0 \rightarrow x = 2$$

If $x = 2$, the picture is restored to 1.0, its original size. Now she can write a similar equation for the problem above:

$$0.833n = 1.0$$

1. So, $n = $ _____.

CARLO'S STRATEGY: Use guess and test.

He knows that to make the picture larger, the machine must be set at a number greater than 1. He tries multiplying 0.833 by 1.5:

$$0.833 \times 1.5 = 1.25$$

He tries a smaller number, 1.1:

$$0.833 \times 1.1 = 0.92$$

Carlo now knows that the setting must be somewhere between 1.1 and 1.5

2. What setting should Carlo guess next? _____

APPLY

A necklace originally sold for $50 at a store. It was put on sale for 10% off. Then it was put on Super Sale for 25% off the sale price. What is the Super Sale price of the necklace?

3. Which strategy will you use? _____

4. What is the price of the necklace? _____

PRACTICE

5. Which of these numbers satisfies both of these inequalities: $x > 4.8$ and $x < 5.2$? _____

   A. $4\frac{3}{4}$ C. $4\frac{5}{6}$

   B. $5\frac{2}{5}$ D. $5\frac{2}{9}$

6. Rusty shared a dinner check with three other people. The bill came to $92 and included a 15% tip. How large a tip did Rusty pay? _____

   A. $12   C. $3

   B. $3.45   D. $6.25?

7. A sheet of paper is 0.008 cm thick. How many sheets would you need to make a stack of paper 1 foot high? _____

8. Identify the digit that each letter stands for. The letter Q = 1. _____

   ```
     B T T A
   + C B T A
   ---------
   Q Q A A A
   ```

THINK ABOUT IT

9. In problems 5–8, which strategy did you end up using? How were you able to solve the problem using this strategy?

   _____
   _____

10. If you were going to explain to someone else how to solve these problems, which strategy would you use? Explain.

    _____
    _____
    _____
    _____

SOLVING COMPLEX PROBLEMS • **99**

Solving Problems When You Forget the Procedure

Sometimes you might forget how to do a problem. You also might forget procedures such as multiplying decimals, finding percents, or dealing with exponents. In cases like these, you can:
- *make a model*
- *use equivalent numbers*

Choose the strategy that works best for you.

LEARN

You may come across a test problem that looks like this:

Order these fractions from least to greatest:

$\frac{7}{8} \quad \frac{11}{12} \quad \frac{5}{6}$

CANDACE'S STRATEGY: Make a model.

She represents the three fractions on these bars.

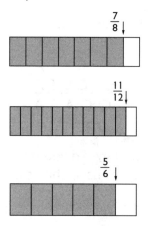

1. Which fraction is largest? _____

JEROME'S STRATEGY: Use equivalent numbers.

He changes each of the three numbers to a decimal by dividing:

$$8\overline{)7.000} = .875 \qquad 12\overline{)11.000} = .91\overline{6} \qquad 6\overline{)5.000} = .8\overline{33}$$

$\frac{7}{8} = .875 \qquad \frac{11}{12} = .91\overline{6} \qquad \frac{5}{6} = .8\overline{33}$

2. Which fraction is smallest? _____

100 • CHOOSING A STRATEGY

APPLY

On Friday, 60% of the 25 town council members voted for a new library. How many people voted for the library?

If you forgot how to find percents you could make a model showing how 60 out of 100 is equivalent to some unknown part of 25. You could also change 60% to a decimal and solve the problem using decimals.

3. Which strategy will you use? _____

4. How many people voted for the new library? _____

PRACTICE

5. What is the average of 4.75; 5.0; and $6\frac{3}{8}$? _____
   - A. $5\frac{3}{4}$
   - B. 5.25
   - C. $5\frac{3}{8}$
   - D. 5.0

6. Paula checked her answers on a fractions test on her calculator. Her calculator gave her an answer of 4.05. As a mixed number in lowest terms, how should Paula expect to see this number represented? _____

7. A single bacterium split to form 2^1 bacteria. Those 2 split to form 2^2 bacteria. The process continued until there were 2^6 bacteria. How many bacteria were there in all? _____

8. What is $a - b$ if $a = {}^-5.7$ and $b = {}^-3\frac{2}{3}$? _____

THINK ABOUT IT

9. Which strategy did you choose for problems 5–8? Why did you choose this strategy?

_____

_____

_____

10. How does making a model help you understand how to solve a problem?

_____

_____

_____

_____

SOLVING PROBLEMS WHEN YOU FORGET THE PROCEDURE

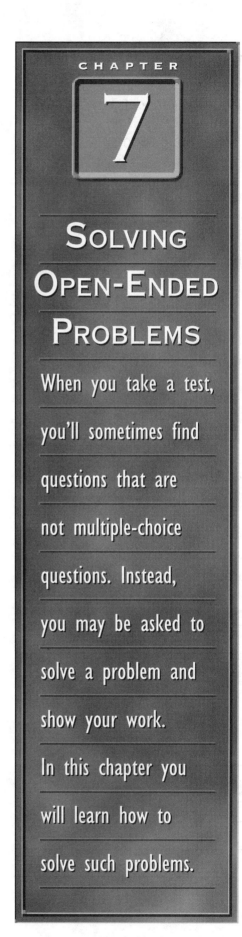

CHAPTER 7

SOLVING OPEN-ENDED PROBLEMS

When you take a test, you'll sometimes find questions that are not multiple-choice questions. Instead, you may be asked to solve a problem and show your work. In this chapter you will learn how to solve such problems.

READING AND SOLVING OPEN-ENDED PROBLEMS

To solve an open-ended problem, work through these steps:

STEP 1: Read the problem.

STEP 2: Explore the problem and plan what to do.

STEP 3: Solve the problem.

STEP 4: Present your answer by showing how you solved it. You may also be asked to explain your thinking as you solved the problem. Be sure to present your solution as clearly as you can. You will be evaluated on how well you explain what you did as well as on your ability to solve the problem.

STEP 5: Look over your answer. Did you answer every part of the question? Does your answer seem clear and complete?

Here's a sample open-ended test problem. The table below shows the way Eva usually spends an 8-hour work day.

Activity	Time
Writing letters	1 hr
Typing	$1\frac{1}{2}$ hr
Answering phones	1 hr
Seeing clients	$2\frac{1}{2}$ hr
Lunch	$\frac{1}{2}$ hr
Meetings	$1\frac{1}{2}$ hr

Draw a graph that compares how long different activities take.

Before you start planning a graph, think carefully about different kinds of graphs and what information each kind shows best.

GRAPH	BEST USE
bar graph	comparing amounts of information
line graph	showing changes in data over time
line plot	showing how data is clustered
circle graph	showing comparative sizes of parts of a whole

The first graph you can probably rule out is the line plot. It won't show the names of the activities.

1. Why might you also be able to rule out a line graph?

   _____

2. You might choose either a bar graph or a circle graph. Which would you choose? Why?

   _____

3. If you made a bar graph, what numbers would you use on the scale? Why?

   _____

4. If you made a circle graph, how would you decide how big each one-hour section in the graph would be? Explain your answer.

   _____

   _____

5. Draw your graph here.

Is your graph complete? Is it labeled correctly? Does it include all of the information in the original table?

READING AND SOLVING OPEN-ENDED PROBLEMS • 103

Exploring and Solving Open-Ended Problems

Sometimes when you read an open-ended problem on a test, you won't know right away how to solve the problem. Try exploring the problem in a couple of ways. Try making an example to guess and test, or try restating the information by making a model, picture, or table. This will give you some new ideas that will help you solve the problem. Remember to mention what you did and why in your explanation.

The time is 12:30 p.m. Gerald and Jill Arno want to go to a movie that starts at 6:00 p.m. They need to complete these tasks first:

1-PERSON TASKS	2-PERSON TASKS
mow lawn—2 hours	wash windows—2 hours per person
laundry—45 minutes	wash dog—$\frac{1}{2}$ hour per person
wash floor—25 minutes	
clean sinks—20 minutes	

- They can borrow a mower and mow the lawn together in 1 hour.
- They need $\frac{1}{2}$ hour to wash and dress and 45 minutes to get to the theater.

How should they divide the tasks so they get everything done and still arrive on time for the show? Show how you found your answer.

If you're not sure what to do, try any guess, and test it. Suppose, for example, that Gerald tries to do all the tasks. You can see that even just the one-person tasks take Gerald to 4:00. Also, this schedule allows no time for washing up, dressing, and traveling to the theater.

GERALD'S SCHEDULE
12:30–2:30—mow lawn
2:30–3:15—laundry
3:15–3:40—wash floor
3:40–4:00—clean sinks
4:00—wash windows

However, your exploration has pointed up two important new questions that are not stated in the problem:

- When should the Arnos stop working and start getting ready?
- How much time do they have from 12:30 to the time they must get ready?

Answering these questions is a good way to get started.

104 • Solving Open-Ended Problems

1. Work backward to find the latest time that the Arnos can stop work. _____

2. To figure out how much time Jill and Gerald have to complete their tasks, find the elapsed time between 12:30 and 4:45. _____

To assign tasks, start with the least flexible demands on Jill and Gerald's time. These are the 2-person tasks. You know that both Jill and Gerald must do these tasks.

3. What is the total time that each person will spend on these tasks?

   $4 \text{ hr } 15 \text{ min} - 2\frac{1}{2} \text{ hr} = 1 \text{ hr } 45 \text{ min}$

   _____

To fill out the list of tasks, use the guess-and-test strategy. Here are two possibilities:

GUESS A

JILL		GERALD	
floor	25 min	lawn	2 hr
laundry	45 min		
sinks	20 min		

GUESS B

JILL		GERALD	
lawn	1 hr	lawn	1 hr
laundry	45 min	floor	25 min
		sinks	20 min

4. Which way will get the jobs done in time? _____

This problem asks you to give a numerical answer and also explain your answer. Go over what you did to solve your problem.

5. How should Jill and Gerald divide the tasks so they get everything done and still arrive on time for the show?

   Jill should do these tasks:

   _____

   Gerald should do these tasks:

   _____

6. Describe in writing the steps you took to arrive at your answer. Think about whether something such as a table or a graph will make your answer clearer.

   _____

   _____

Is your answer clear? Is it complete?

EXPLORING AND SOLVING OPEN-ENDED PROBLEMS • **105**

PRACTICE SOLVING OPEN-ENDED PROBLEMS

Here is a chance to practice solving an open-ended problem to prepare you for tests. Remember the steps you should use to solve any problem:

STEP 1: Read the problem.

STEP 2: Explore the problem and plan what to do.

STEP 3: Solve the problem.

STEP 4: Present your answer by writing about what you did and why you did it. Be sure to present your solution as clearly as you can.

STEP 5: Look over your answer.

At the end of the lesson, you'll have a chance to evaluate how well you did.

There are two ways to save at the Songs 'n' Sounds chain of stores.

Does one coupon give a better deal? If so, which one? Give reasons to support your answer. Your reasons could include one or more specific examples.

Begin solving the problem by using a guess-and-test strategy.

1. Which coupon would give you a better deal if you wanted to get only one $10.00 CD?

   _____

2. Which coupon is better if you wanted to get two $20.00 CDs?

   _____

106 • SOLVING OPEN-ENDED PROBLEMS

3. Plan other examples that you need to test.

_____
_____
_____

SOLVE THE PROBLEM

4. Do the calculations that you need in order to solve your problem. Show your work here.

```
┌─────────────────────────────────────────────┐
│                                             │
│                                             │
│                                             │
│                                             │
│                                             │
│                                             │
└─────────────────────────────────────────────┘
```

PRESENT YOUR ANSWER

5. Does one coupon give a better deal? State and explain your opinion. Include examples that illustrate your reasons.

_____
_____
_____
_____
_____

THINK ABOUT IT

Evaluate your answer. Use this checklist.

☐ Did you answer the question that was asked?

☐ Did you show the process or the calculations that you used to arrive at the answer?

☐ Was your written explanation presented in a clear way?

☐ If necessary, did you use examples such as graphs, schedules, or specific situations?

Open-Ended Problems Test

Use the steps that you learned in this chapter to help you solve these problems. Most of the problems have more than one part. You may need the information from one part to solve the next. Use another paper if you need space. You have one hour to finish the test.

Problem 1

What number is this?
- Its square root is a prime number.
- It is between 100 and 300.
- The sum of its digits is an odd number.

Explain in the space below how you arrived at your answer. Continue on another paper if you need to.

PROBLEM 2

This map shows the highways through Calabash County and the distance in miles between towns. Use the map to answer the questions below. Use additional paper if necessary.

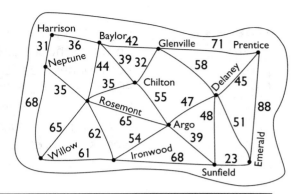

A.

Mirella travels for her business. She is planning to drive from Harrison to Sunfield. She will stop at each town she passes through. If she starts at Harrison and travels to Sunfield through Neptune, Willow, and Ironwood, what will be the average number of miles that she drives between each town?

B.

What is the shortest route from Harrison to Sunfield? Describe in writing how you ruled out other answers. Continue your explanation on another paper if you need to.

PROBLEM 3

Randy and Jamal are runners on their school track team. Both runners specialize in the 400-meter race. Each boy kept a record of the times at which he ran during one week's practice sessions. The times are all in seconds.

	MORNING PRACTICE	AFTERNOON PRACTICE
Randy	48.7 48.8 48.7 49.1 48.4	48.5 48.7 49.1 49.2 48.6
Jamal	48.5 48.3 48.3 64.5* 48.2	48.3 48.2 48.4 48.5 48.1
	*fell in this race	

A. What is Randy's mean time? What is Jamal's mean time?

B. Whose mean time was faster in afternoon practices? Who had a faster overall mean time?

C. Which athlete seems to have the better overall record? Explain your answer. Continue on another paper if you need to.

PROBLEM 4

Terence and Vera work in the sales departments of differe[nt] stores. Terence earns: $450 a week plus 2% of any amount [he sells.] Vera earns: $350 a week plus 4% of any amount she sells.

A. Suppose Terence sells $1,500 worth of clothing in one w[eek.] Vera also sells $1,500 worth of clothing in that week. Wh[o earns] more that week? How much more does that person earn?

B. One week, Terence and Vera each make the same dollar sales of clothing. They each earn exactly the same amount (including salary and commission). What is the amount of *sales* that each person makes that week?

C. Suppose Terence and Vera have the same dollar sales for one week. What can you tell about whether Terence or Vera earned more money? Give a written explanation telling how you figured out your answer. Continue on another paper if you need to.

PROBLEM 4

Terence and Vera work in the sales departments of different clothing stores. Terence earns: $450 a week plus 2% of any amount he sells. Vera earns: $350 a week plus 4% of any amount she sells.

A. Suppose Terence sells $1,500 worth of clothing in one week. Vera also sells $1,500 worth of clothing in that week. Who earns more that week? How much more does that person earn?

B. One week, Terence and Vera each make the same dollar sales of clothing. They each earn exactly the same amount (including salary and commission). What is the amount of *sales* that each person makes that week?

C. Suppose Terence and Vera have the same dollar sales for one week. What can you tell about whether Terence or Vera earned more money? Give a written explanation telling how you figured out your answer. Continue on another paper if you need to.